# 精养父母

## Parent-supporting: A Chinese Family's Way

### 实验报告

高 鸣 著
Written by Gao Ming

张 宏  姜琪瑶 译
Translated by  Zhang Hong  Jiang Qiyao

文汇出版社

艳而脱俗，群又超凡。
　　　　　——陈述

**Beautiful in a raffish kind of way; unusual
and unsophisticated in a plain sense.**
　　　　　　　　　　——**Chen Shu**

# 妻子的话　值与不值

高鸣告诉我,他要写一本我如何孝敬父母的书,开始我很反对,认为不值一提。不值有三:一来孝敬父母天经地义,乃常识;二来我未觉孝敬之事有何过人之处,甚至觉得还有不周到的地方,甚惭愧;三来雷锋做好事尚不留名,我岂可自说自话,自卖自夸。

高鸣认为不然。他反举了值得有三:一来常识也要普及,否则大部分教育都成了废话;二来孝敬之人大有,但孝敬之法未必相同,可以推广讨论;三来与时俱进,如今做好事也要宣传,否则宣传的都是坏人坏事,社会就没有丰富的声音。好比西方一个法案出台,反对者游行,赞成者也得游行。

女儿说,爸爸妈妈说得都有道理,那就写出来给大家评一评。

我们家民主,二比一,少数服从多数,此书遂成。

朱艳群

# The Wife's Words: Worthwhile or Not

I strongly opposed the idea when Gao Ming mentioned to me his plan of writing about how I tried my best to be a filial daughter to my parents, for I think that what I have done so far isn't worthy a book. This opposition comes out of three reasons. First, it is common sense and God's truth that one should well treat and honor his parents. Second, I don't think what I have done to my parents deserves any compliments as other daughters would do the same, let alone there are times that I was not that considerate enough in taking care of them. And last but not least, as the good guy Lei Feng would not leave behind his name after he had done his good deeds, how can I blow my own trumpet?

Gao Ming took it the other way. He raised three reasons to show why it was worthwhile to write the book. First, common sense needs to be popularized or otherwise most of the teaching ends up in nonsense. Second, there are numerous people who are good to their parents, but the ways people take towards their parents are different, therefore it is necessary to spread them for discussion. And last, the trend nowadays is that doing good should also be publicized. If what people hear are all those bad guys and the bad deeds they commit, no rich voices will be broadcast in the society. It is of no difference to the introduction of a new bill in some western countries—the opponents will go on demonstration to oppose while the supporters will also go on demonstration to back it.

My daughter made her comments: well, you both have the reason there, then why don't you write the book and invite the readers to voice their opinions?

Ours is a democracy family. The vote is two to one and the one obeys. And hence the book you are reading now.

Zhu Yanqun

# 女儿的话　预习未来

在很长的时间里,我家常住人口是四个,爸爸、妈妈、外婆和我。爸爸妈妈是中坚力量,里里外外都要抓,我和外婆,一对老小,是他们"养"的对象。养我,养得挺好,有《精养女儿实验报告》为证;养外婆,养得也很好,有这本《精养父母实验报告》为证。

此书将养外婆的经历写成 50 个小故事,既是回忆,更是心得的整理。我多年来与爸爸妈妈和外婆生活在一起,日子过得很和谐、很幸福。读了爸爸的这本书,我仿佛找到了和谐的规律,遵照此法,接下来的 50 年、100 年都可以这样幸福下去。

赡养父母是传统。在我家这个崇尚民主自由的环境里,赡养父母不是为传统而传统,而是有强烈的个人动因,也就是说,赡养父母是我们内心觉得很有好处,非常乐意做的事情。很多人以为,孩子代表希望和未来,而老人是过时的,没有剩余价值的,所以重视孩子而轻视老人。其实对于我们每一个具体的个人而言,情况往往相反。孩子是自己的过去,老人是自己的将来。在孩子身上,我们重新感知一个生命逐渐成熟的过程,仿佛重新成长一遍,是"复习"。而我们的将来会如何,只能在老人身上体会,老人让我们"预习"未来。对学习来说,复习和预习一样重要;对于人生,孩子和老人一样重要。

历史上、社会上孝顺老人的好子女不乏其人，可歌可泣的例子不少，爸爸之所以写下这本《精养父母实验报告》，一是有感于妈妈可贵的善良孝顺之心，二是对于妈妈孝顺外婆的细节和方法大为赞赏，称其不是普通的赡养，而是"精养"。在我看来，无论对孩子还是老人，"精养"的目的就是帮助一个人完整地生活，而不是替代或者阻碍。

孩子，不会吃不会走的时候，我们要喂食要抱着走，他们长大了，我们就要锻炼他们独立思考的能力，培养他们的情商，给他们做事的机会，总之，让他们有能力尽早掌控自己的生活是最快乐的，而父母，就是要让这种快乐最大化。

老人，老病至衣食皆需人料理的最后阶段，需要子女悉心照顾一如婴儿，之前的时光，长则几十年，他们虽然很多方面已经逐渐落后于年轻人，但是大多数人仍有一颗年轻的心，他们愿意学习，乐意分担，他们甚至比年轻人更希望自己"中用"，因此，让他们觉得自己"还很行"是最快乐的，而子女，就是要让这种快乐最大化。

这本书的很多故事都是让外婆变得"很行"或者让她觉得自己"很行"的，个中趣味，令人莞尔。

妈妈不但给了外婆丰富而愉快的精神生活，还为我们全家创造了优渥的物质生活。今年已经89岁的老外婆住在漂亮的大房子里，做着喜欢的事情，有求必应，她的幸福感染了我们所有人。我可以很负责任地说，外婆的今天就是妈妈的明天，妈妈这种身体力行的教育是最好的榜样，她未来的老年生活也会像外婆一样非常幸福。

爸爸在这本书中充当了一个记录者，他把功劳都记在妈妈头上了，其实爸爸也是个好同志。

**高韵冽**

# The Daughter's Words: Preview the Future

For a fairly long period, there are four members living together in my family. They are my dad, my mom, my maternal grandma and I. The backbone of my family is my dad and mom, for they need to take care of both their work and the family chores at the same time, while the old and the little ones, my grandma and I, are the people they must raise and support. My parents have well-raised me and there is evidence to prove what I say here, the book *Daughter-rearing: A Chinese Family's Way*. My parents have also well-supported my grandma and there too is evidence to prove this, the book *Parent-supporting: A Chinese Family's Way*, which is right in front of you now.

This book contains fifty small stories covering the undergoing of how my parents, my mum in particular, support my grandma. There are both recollections as well as what we have learned in the process. I have long enjoyed a happy and harmonious life with my parents and my grandma. After reading what dad has written in this book, it seems that I have found the rules for harmony and I can continue to enjoy this happiness for the next fifty or a hundred years as long as I follow them in my own life.

It is a long cherished Chinese tradition to wait on and support one's parents. In a family like ours that goes for democracy and freedom, it is out of strong personal motivations rather than tradition that we wait on and honor parents. That is to say, waiting on parents is something that we feel beneficial inside and something we are always ready to do. Many people hold the concept that children represent the future and hope, while old people are behind the times with no surplus values and therefore they attach much importance to their children and show indifference to the old people. In fact it is just the opposite to every one of us as an individual person. The children are the showcase of our past while the old people are the samples of our future. We can perceive the process of the ripening of a life from the children as if we are re-growing once again—it is a "review". However, what we are going to become in the future can only be sensed or tasted from the old people. It's the old people who would make us "preview" our future. It is of the same significance to review and to preview in learning. While in one life, children and old people are equally important.

Such people are not rare in history as well as in the society who try their best to wait upon and support their parents, and neither are the touching stories of these people. I believe my dad wrote this *Parent-supporting: A Chinese Family's Way* because he has been deeply moved by my mom's commendable kindness and filial piety towards her mother, as well as has appreciated her ways and methods to wait on my grandma. He has called them ways of "intensive culture" instead of "plain support". To me, the aim of "intensive culture", whether to children or old people, is to help a person to live a whole life, and not to replace or block it.

When children are unable to eat by themselves or walk on their own, we have to feed them and hold them. When they grow up, we need to train their independent thinking power and cultivate their emotional quotient and provide them with opportunities as well. Whole on whole, we should help them master the ability to manage their own life as soon as possible so that they can enjoy the happiness of life. And parents'role is to maximize this happiness.

And the old people require their offspring's meticulous care-taking when they come to the ripe stage of life, weak and ailing, and need people to feed them and clothe them like babies. For many years before this, most of them still keep with them a young heart to learn, to share, and to hope themselves to be even more "useful" than the young people, though throughout the days they have gradually lacked behind the young people in many aspects. So to help them feel themselves "quite well and capable" is the happiest thing to them. And the role of the sons and daughters is to maximize this happiness as well.

Many of the stories in this book are about how my grandma was made to become "able to do something" or to feel "capable of something". We often can't help smiling by the fun and interest in them.

Mom has not only enriched grandma's happy life but also created a well-off material life for the whole family. Now my eighty-nine year old grandma lives in a big beautiful house, does whatever she likes to do. Her requests are fully satisfied while all of us are infected with her happiness. I think it's safe to say that what my grandma enjoys today shall be enjoyed by my mom tomorrow. The teaching done by my mom with what she does has set up the best model in the world. I can assure that her old-age life in the future will be as happy as my grandma's.

My dad plays the role of a recorder. He has given the credit all to my mom despite the fact that my dad himself is such a commendable guy as well.

Gao Yunlie

# 自序　孝是天职

邓小平说："不管黑猫白猫，会捉老鼠的就是好猫。"反过来说，不捉老鼠的猫就是坏猫。为什么以捉不捉老鼠作为评判猫的唯一依据？答案是，捉老鼠是猫的天职。可见，别的什么事可做可不做，唯有天职，是非尽不可的，否则，就是坏。

在家庭里，对下养育子女，对上孝敬父母，是人的天职。在当今的中国社会，父母尽养育子女之天职似乎不成问题，成问题的是子女孝敬父母之天职，不尽之人大有。

父母生养了儿女，儿女孝敬父母天经地义。父母的生和养，对于子女来说，是最大的恩。有恩不报，如同欠债不还，有恩不报，有债不还，不合情理，在人间行不通。如果一个社会，不尽孝敬父母之天职的人越来越多，这个社会是有危险的，因为长此以往，成年人会失却生儿育女的动因。为了传宗接代生育的人不多，生育者大多是为了养儿防老和天伦之乐。假如生育之前便知晓儿女日后孝敬将落空，防老和天伦之乐子虚乌有，则生育的积极性必将降至接近于零。如此这般，人类将后继无人。

不捉老鼠的猫不是好猫，不孝敬父母的人不是好人。朱艳群精养父母，是个好女人。

谨以此书献给天下父母及子女，并恭祝岳母90大寿。

高　鸣

# The Bounden Duty of Human Being: Filial Piety

Mr. Deng Xiaoping once commented, "It doesn't matter if a cat is white or black, as long as it catches the mouse." If we put it in the opposite way, we can say that a cat is a bad one if it doesn't catch the mouse. How come that the ability to catch mouse has become the only criterion for judging a cat? The answer is inevitable as it is the cat's bounden duty to catch mouse. In this sense it is quite clear that there are things that people can or cannot do at their will except one, that is, their bounden duty in life. Otherwise they are not different from the undutiful cat that can't catch the mouse.

It is then one's bounden duty in a family to raise children and support parents. In present day China, it doesn't seem to be a problem for parents to carry out their duty of taking care of their children. However, it does have become a problem as quite many people now neglect their duty of looking after their parents.

It is all justified for sons and daughters to support their parents as they give life to them. Parents' efforts to give birth to and raise them are deemed to be the greatest benevolence ever obliged on them. It is therefore unreasonable for people not to return the favor to their parents just like they do not pay back the debt they owe to someone. This won't be accepted in the world.

A society with increasing number of people who are not carrying out their duty of taking care of their parents is one in danger, for in the long run such would lead to the loss of the motivation for adults to bear children. There are not many people who give birth to children for the purpose of carrying on the family line, yet quite many tend to bring up children to support themselves in their old age as well as to enjoy the cheers of family relationships. However, their initiatives will be reduced almost to nil if they know their old-age support and family happiness will come to nothing before they give birth to children. If such will be the case, then human beings will have no successors in the future.

It is not a good cat if one doesn't catch the mouse, and someone is not a dutiful person if one doesn't support one's parents in old age. Zhu Yanqun has done all she can to take good care of her parents. And she is a good woman.

This book is dedicated to all the parents and their children in the world, and to my mother-in-law's ninetieth birthday.

Gao Ming

# 目录

1 妻子的话　值与不值
　The Wife's Words: Worthwhile or Not　　　　2

4 女儿的话　预习未来
　The Daughter's Words: Preview the Future　　6

9 自序　孝是天职
　The Bounden Duty of Human Being:Filial Piety　10

001 差点饿死
　　Nearly Starved to Death　　　　　　　　003

005 半粒喜糖
　　Half a Wedding Candy　　　　　　　　　007

009 夏天的扇子冬天的手
　　A Summer Fan and Two Winter Hands　　010

012 挽着妈散步
　　Taking Walks Arm in Arm　　　　　　　013

015 送父母一套房
　　An Apartment for Parents　　　　　　　017

019 报喜不报忧
　　No Bad News but Good Ones　　　　　　021

024 听母亲说从前的事
　　Stories About the Past Told by Mum　　026

028 乘飞机
　　Taking Flights　　　　　　　　　　　029

**031**  说"乌托邦"
"Utopia"                                                032

**034**  88 岁的观众
An Eighty-eight-year Old Movie-goer        035

**037**  夸妈妈
Complimenting Mum                            038

**040**  给妈读报
Reading Newspaper to Mum                  042

**044**  双重标准
Double Standard                                    046

**048**  瓜子和胡桃
Sunflower Seeds and Walnuts                049

**051**  带妈上班
Taking Mum to Work                              052

**054**  帮妈找"伴"
Looking for "Partners" for Mum              055

**057**  写毛笔字画画
Brush Writing and Painting                      058

**060**  学英语
Learning English                                    061

**063**  让母亲当"文秘"
Hiring Mum as The "Secretary"              065

**067**  生日感言
Birthday Speech                                    069

**071**  首月工资
Salary of The First Month                       072

**074**  朱艳群洗头
Hair-washing                                        076

| | | |
|---|---|---|
| 078 | "上得厅堂"<br>"Up in the Hall" | 079 |
| 081 | 甜口良药<br>Sweet Good Medicine | 082 |
| 084 | 朱艳群读书<br>Zhu Yanqun's Preference in Reading Books | 086 |
| 088 | 母亲的衣服<br>Clothes for Mum | 090 |
| 092 | 鸟语花香<br>Singing Birds and Fragrant Flowers | 093 |
| 095 | 给玩具<br>Offering Toys | 097 |
| 099 | 泡电话<br>Hooked on the Phone | 100 |
| 102 | 打麻将<br>Playing Mah-jong | 103 |
| 105 | 父母的小店<br>Parents' Store | 106 |
| 108 | 接送车<br>Courtesy Cars | 109 |
| 111 | 发呆房<br>A Room for Sitting Idle | 112 |
| 114 | 轮椅和轿子<br>The Wheelchair and The Sedan-chair | 115 |
| 117 | 看话剧<br>Watching the Stage Play | 119 |
| 121 | 一种游戏<br>A Game | 122 |

124 "老人房"
Rooms for the Old                126

128 三陪母亲
Escort to Mum in Three Ways      130

132 下午茶
Afternoon Tea                    134

136 养鸡
Keeping Chicken                  138

140 种菜如养花
Raising Vegetables as Flowers    141

143 共同语言
A Common Language                145

147 让父母作点主
Leaving Decisions to Parents     149

151 母亲的远亲
Mum's Distant Relatives          153

155 不一样的饼
Cakes of Difference              156

158 甜食的功能
The Functions of Desserts        159

161 取名
Giving Names                     162

164 替母购书
Buying Books for Mum             165

167 松散的大家庭
A Big Loosely-structured Family  168

170 照相
Photo-taking                     172

# 差点饿死

人无完人，人难免犯错，由人掌控的国家也难免犯错。上个世纪 50 年代批判马寅初，鼓励生育，致使人口暴涨，就是国家犯错。全国人民吃大锅饭，致使大众没了劳动积极性，也是国家犯错。吃饭的人多了，创造的财富又少，国家和老百姓就贫穷，在相当一段时期内，全中国饿死了不少人。1958 年出生的妻——朱艳群算是幸运，小时候没有饿死，却是差点饿死。

朱艳群上有两个哥哥，一个姐姐，是父母最小的孩子。朱艳群说，她差点饿死的时候还年幼，饿了只有生理反应和条件反射，只会哭，心里不会难受，心灵不会受创伤，长大以后也没阴影。差点饿死是自己 8 岁那年，母亲亲口告诉她的。当年全家饥寒交迫，为了补贴家用，母亲走街串户去别人家做裁缝，没时间带尚在婴儿期的小女儿，只能把她寄放在托儿所。小镇上所谓的托儿所，简易得很，仅有一间旧屋，几张硬板床，一个照看孩子的老太，并无食物供应。母亲自己吃不饱，奶水几近于无，又买不起奶粉之类，故每天早上喂点粥汤就送去托儿所。饿极的小艳群，长哭不止，先是大哭，哭不动就小哭，就泣不成声。照看的老太一筹莫展，有时慷慨地把自己家中带来的咸菜放一点在艳群的口中，聊胜于无。母亲曾多次含着眼泪带着歉意对朱艳群说，每当傍晚放工时去托儿所接她，总是怀有一种恐惧,生怕看到的是已经饿死的女儿。幸而,瘦弱无比、满眼是泪的小艳群,总还有奄奄一息。

　　朱艳群告诉我,8岁那年听了自己差点饿死的故事,不知为什么,她丝毫没有生出对父母的抱怨和责怪,相反,就在那一刻起,她开始有了怜惜父母的心。她想,在那贫困的年代,由于她的出生和存在,一定是给父母增添了更多的艰难。她想,父母都是深爱着自己每一个孩子的,当他们恐惧自己的女儿有可能会饿死的时候,心情是何等地痛苦!基于这样的想法,她从小立志长大以后要有所能力,有所出息,从主观到客观,做一个孝敬父母的女儿。

# Nearly Starved to Death

To err, human. That's why people tend to make mistakes, and so do the countries which are run by people. In the fifties last century, professor Ma Yinchu, who first advocated the idea of birth control in China, was widely criticized and the country made a big mistake to carry out the policy of encouraging child-bearing. It was also the government's mistake to carry out "the egalitarian practice of everybody eating from the same big pot" which at the time made people in the country lose their initiatives to work. With more people born and less fortune created, the country and its people were poverty stricken, which resulted in the death of many people in hunger in the span of a couple of years. My wife Zhu Yanqun, who was born in 1958, is lucky enough as she didn't starve to death when she was a small child. But she almost died of hunger.

Zhu Yanqun is the youngest of the four children in her family, with two elder brothers and one elder sister. She said she was very small when she was almost starved to death. Out of physical response and conditioned reflex caused by hunger, she kept crying and crying was the only thing she could do then. But this left no psychological impact on her. It was when she was eight that her mother told her the story. In that year the whole family was suffering from hunger and cold. To earn some subsidy for the family, her mother went out to work as a tailor and left her baby daughter in the care of a nursery. The nursery in a small town at the time was very shabby and insufficiently equipped: an old house with several hard beds, with an old nanny looking after the children, no food provided. Her mother can hardly have food for herself, and therefore had almost no milk to nurse her daughter. She could not afford the powdered milk either so every morning she could only feed the baby daughter with some porridge soup before sending her to the nursery. The little Yanqun was so hungry that she cried and cried till she was exhausted and then she sobbed and sobbed till no sound was heard. The old nanny could not find any way to ease her and sometimes could only put a little bit of the preserved pickles she brought with her into the baby's mouth. For many times and with tears in eyes, her mother has told Yanqun apologetically that she was filled with fear every time she went to pick up her at dusk, for fear that she would find her daughter already dead of hunger. Fortunately it always turned out that the skinny tearful little baby Yanqun was still breathing.

Zhu Yanqun said to me that, just out of no reason, she did not have the least complaint or grumble about her parents the moment she was told the story of starvation at the age of eight. On the contrary, right from that moment on, she started to feel tender and protective toward her parents. She thought that it must have added to her father and mother lot of hardship when she came to this world and survived in that impoverished times. Every parent is in deep love with every of their own child. And what pain they must have endured when they were in great fear of the possibility of their daughter's death of starvation! With this mentality she has resolved ever since to make something of herself when she grows up and to well support and take good care of her parents both materially and emotionally.

# 半粒喜糖

锦上添花总不如雪中送炭,父母对孩子亦如是。

我问朱艳群,你常说小时候母亲对你们几个孩子非常好,究竟如何好法?她深情地说:"试举一例吧:记得我5岁那年,母亲出席邻居的婚宴,席间得到两粒喜糖。母亲没舍得吃,回家后将两粒喜糖二分为四,分给四个孩子各人半粒。这半粒喜糖真是又甜又苦啊!甜的是难得有糖吃,嘴馋,糖分外甜;苦的是,可怜父母心。为了这半粒喜糖,数十年来回忆起,不知生出了多少对父母的感激之情。"

常言道:"滴水之恩当涌泉相报。"父母给了子女以生命,以养和育,又岂止滴水之恩呢?可惜的是,生活中常有父母给了子女"涌泉之恩",却得不到"滴水之报"。笔者有一个文友,前不久伤心地向我诉苦,他把儿子辛辛苦苦养大,四年前又送去国外读大学,花费了所有的积蓄,不料即将回国的儿子非但毫不感恩,反而在电话中连声抱怨父母没当大官没发大财,没为他备有一份像样的家产和一个让他大展宏图的平台。笔者另有一个商友对我说,女儿新嫁,他送了一辆价值50万元的VOLVO,谁知女儿不领情,还哭着说她的小姐妹新近也嫁,父母送的是100多万元的宝马。

妻——朱艳群对上述两例大有感慨,她说:"我小时候和父母是有苦同当,易;如今的家长和子女是有福同享,难啊!"她接着又说:"我们人到中年生活好过了,有福了,可要和已经老年的父母有福也同享,唯有如此,心里才安,才踏实。"我是见证人,朱艳群对母亲的好胜过对女儿的好。这一点正好与如今的大多数人相反,现在的大多数对子女的好胜过对父母的好,而且胜过许多许多。

# Half a Wedding Candy

It is always better for people to provide firewood in frozen days than to put icing on the cake. The same is the case with parents and children.

I once asked Zhu Yanqun, "You often say that your mother was very nice to the four of you when you were very young. How nice that nice was?" She responded affectionately, "I'll give you an example. When I was five, I remember that mother attended a neighbor's wedding and received two candies at the feast. She didn't eat them and took back home to cut them into four and gave each of us half a candy. This half candy tasted both sweet and bitter. It was sweet because we rarely had candies while it was bitter because it contained my parents' love and devotion to us. Every time I recall this half happy candy in the past decades, there always gush out in my heart tons of gratitude toward my parents."

The old saying has it that a drop of grace should be requited with a surge spring. The parents have given life to the children and have brought them up as well. In the process, how many drops of grace have fallen on the children? Unfortunately, life does not always follow the old saying and more than often parents' surge of spring grace will not be requited with a drop from their children in return. I have a literary friend who not long ago bitterly aired his grievances to me. He raised his son in all the hardships and sent him to study abroad four years ago, costing all his savings. Out of his surprise, the soon-to-return son showed no gratitude at all. Instead, he complained to his parents in the phone call that they did not accumulate for him a handsome property and prepare for him a business to realize his ambition. Another business friend told me that when recently his daughter got married, he bought her a 500000 yuan worth VOLVO as wedding gift. His daughter did not appreciate his kindness at all and cried instead and said that a friend of hers got an over one million yuan worth BMW from her parents.

My wife Zhu Yanqun sighed at hearing the two stories. She said, "It was quite easy for me as a small child to take over the difficulties together with my parents. But it is real hard for today's parents to share the fortunes with children." She continued. "We begin to enjoy a fairly well-off life in our middle ages and this well-off life should be enjoyed together with our old-aged parents. And only by so doing can we rest at ease." As a witness, I dare to testify that Zhu Yanqun looks after her mother much better than our daughter. This is quite different from most people for nowadays they take far more better care of their children than that of their parents.

# 夏天的扇子冬天的手

有了感恩,离报恩就不远了。

俗话说,养儿防老。此话的意思似乎是说,养育子女,父母年轻和中年的时候纯粹是责任和义务,只有到了老年,才有回报。其实,优秀的子女,从小就会对父母有所孝敬、有所贡献的,未必要等到子女成人,父母老去。

听奶奶说,我爷爷9岁的时候就在船上为10多个人做饭了,分担了家长的劳务。在国际机场,常常见到七八岁的外国小孩,一手拉着比自己更小的小孩,一手拖着行李箱,跟在父母的身后。据说,犹太人从小就会做生意,会帮父母挣钱贴补家用。现在许多中学生、大学生在家不干家务,许多新婚的男女,儿子不养爹,孙子吃爷爷。究其原因,是教育的失败,是父母把孩子宠坏了。

妻——朱艳群也是一个从小就会对父母好的孝敬之人。她父亲在一家杂货店当营业员,每月只有26元的工资,母亲没有固定工作,靠做裁缝打短工挣钱。为了养活一家人,只要有活干,母亲总是不分日夜,不分寒冬酷暑,忙个不停。当年没有空调,干裁缝活冬天难耐寒,夏天难熬热。此情此景,不足10岁的小艳群主动上场了,酷热的夏天,她会拿个把扇子不停地替妈妈"扇风",寒冷的冬天,她会用自己稍微暖和的小手去温热妈妈冰冷的大手。一年又一年,一天又一天,这夏天的扇子冬天的手,成了两幅美丽而动人的图画,成了街头巷尾人们谈论的佳话。

# A Summer Fan and Two Winter Hands

If one feels grateful to somebody, it is not far for him to requite his gratitude.

One old saying says that the purpose of raising sons is to support one in the old age. This sentence seems to imply that it is out of pure obligation for the parents to raise their children when they are in youth and midlife, and that return can only be received in their old ages. As a matter of fact, those sons and daughters of good qualities tend to contribute something to and wait on their parents from their childhood. It does not necessarily happen until the children grow up and the parents are aging.

I was told by my grandma that my grandpa began to share part of his parents' work by cooking for over a dozen people who worked on a ship. From time to time many foreign kids of seven or eight years old can often be seen in many international airports dragging their baggage with one hand and holding their younger sibling with another, following their parents to the boarding gate. It is said that Jews learn to do business and earn money for parents to subsidize their family at an early age. While now in our country many middle school and college students don't do house chores at home, many newly-wed couples do not support their parents and grandchildren rely on their grandparents for financial support. The cause for all this, I believe, lies in the failure of our education, and in the fact that the children are spoiled by the parents.

My wife Zhu Yanqun has shown her dutiful heart towards her parents ever since her childhood. Her father worked as a grocery shop assistant, earning a monthly wage of 26 yuan, while her mother did not have a job and made a living by working as a casual tailor. To support the whole family, her mother worked day and night, no matter whether it was summer or winter and whenever there was tailor work to do. There was no air conditioning those days so the cold in winter and the heat in summer were all beyond the diligent tailors. At this scene, the little nearly-10-year-old Yanqun began to offer her helping hand by cooling her mum with a fan in the extremely hot summer days and warming her mother's cold big hands with her warm little hands in severe cold days. Day after day and year after year, the summer fan and the winter hands turned into two beautiful touching pictures and became a moving story on everybody's lips.

## 挽着妈散步

如今的世道，养狗成风。在国外，常见老外拉着狗一起跑步；在国内，屡见国人牵着狗一起散步。在我们家，妻——朱艳群，常挽着妈出门散步。

有首歌，歌名叫《常回家看看》，说的是已成年的子女，独立生活以后，组成小家庭以后，别忘了养育自己的父母，该常回家——回到父母家，看看自己的长辈。有些人也许实在太忙，难于抽身常回家看看，但我想，至少那些有闲情牵着狗散步的人，应该是有时间"常回家"的，遗憾的是，他们中的一部分，宁愿多和狗在一起。

妻——朱艳群，实在也是一个忙忙碌碌的人，上班要主管公司的事，下班要下厨房做家务。可她说，再忙，也不耽误陪妈散步呀。吃过晚饭，和妈一起散散步，既可以在散步时和妈聊聊天，说说家长里短，宽慰妈妈，也可以消消食，锻炼身体，放松心情，何乐而不为呢？

笔者和自己的母亲没住在一起，陪她散步的机会自然少了，实在是一个遗憾。我想，我要尽可能说服她搬来同住，变"常回家看看"为"常住在一起"，到时，一起散步就可成为"家常便饭"。记得去年陪母亲沿着无锡五里湖走一圈，既是散步，又是观赏一路湖光山色。路遇一位交情甚深的大学同学，他大有感慨地对我说，现在陪老婆孩子或者情人游山玩水的多，难得你能陪老妈出来游玩。我当下意识到，不是我做得怎么好，而是别的一些人做得不够好。比起我的妻子，这方面我还有很大的差距。

# Taking Walks Arm in Arm

It's a trend worldwide nowadays for people to keep pet dogs. Often foreigners are seen jogging with their dogs in other countries, and people here are seen taking a walk with theirs. In our family, my wife Zhu Yanqun usually takes her mother for a walk arm in arm.

There is a pop song titled *Go Home often to Visit our Parents* which is about a piece of advice given to the grown-up children who have left their parents to set up their own families. The song advocates that people should never forget their parents and should go home often to visit their parents and other elders. Some people may be too busy to go home to see their parents, but I believe that those who have the time to walk with their pet dogs should be able to spare some of their time to "go home" from time to time. The pity is that some of them would rather stay with their dogs instead.

My wife Zhu Yanqun is indeed a busy person as she has to take care of her company business at work and do the cooking and other house chores off work at home. However, as she said once, it is never too busy to spare the time taking a stroll with one's mother. There are quite many benefits taking a walk together with mother after dinner, like chatting with her about what happened in the day, comforting her with good news, while at the same time it helps digest and get some exercises and even relax oneself. Why not do this as often as possible?

As I do not live with my mother, it is a great pity that there are very few opportunities for me to take a walk with her. I plan to persuade my mother to move in and live with us so that I can change the "go home often" pattern into "live together" pattern. Till then I believe that I shall be able to take her for a walk at a regular basis. I still remember that one day last year I accompanied my mother to walk around the Wuli Lake to enjoy the natural beauty. During the stroll, we bumped into a good friend of mine at college and he sighed, "It is quite hard to come by that one takes his mother for a walk for now there are more people to take their wife and children or even their mistresses sightseeing." I realized right then that it was not that I did a better job rather that some other people did not do well at all. And by contrast, my wife has done much better than I.

# 送父母一套房

今天的中国,固然有这样那样的问题,西方国家还在拿我们的人权和民主说事,但男女平等这一条,世人有目共睹,中国在地球上是领先的。

在我们家,却是做到了夫妻平等。

家里重要一点的事,夫妻双方都不独裁,总是商量着来,一时统一不起来的,就拖一拖等一等,或者采取"中庸之道",折中着办。可是1999年,在没有征得我同意的情况下,朱艳群花50万元,替她父母在惠山脚下买了套商品房。事后她告知我时做了如下解释:1. 她深知我不会反对替岳父母购房。2. 这件事我万一有异议,她也全然不顾了。由此可见,送父母一套房,是她铁了心要办的事,不惜打破我俩遇要事必商量的潜规则。

上世纪80年代我和朱艳群成婚的时候,处的是计划经济时代,市面上没有商品房一说,住房一律由单位分配。60平方米的住房,3口之家的小家庭住住尚可,再让老年人住在一起,实有不便之处,所以长期以来一直是在市里为从农村来的妻的父母租用了一套住房。让父母在租来的房子里住,朱艳群总是心有不忍,也心有不甘,待到我们开店、开公司赚了些钱,又赶上市场经济了,有商品房可买了,她就迫不及待地为父母买起房来了。

据媒体报道,有些地方选拔干部要考察其对父母是否孝敬,意思是,孝的人不一定能成为好干部,但不孝的人肯定成不了好干部。理由是,一个人对父母都不好,怎么可能对人民好。同理可得,一个女人如果不是一个好女儿,怎么可能成为一个好妻子。我把妻送父母房子看成是对父母好的重要表现,正如她所预料的,我没有异议。其实,我不仅是没有异议,而且是从内心里赞赏的。

民间有个说法:"棒头上出孝子,筷头上出逆子。"话是说得绝对了些,然道理是有几分的。"穷人之家出孝子",穷和孝之间大概也有几分内在联系吧。妻和我结婚时因娘家穷,未有嫁妆,而嫁出去的女儿没有像泼出去的水,给了父母从精神到物质的回报,从这个意义上说,朱艳群也算是出息了。

# An Apartment for Parents

Though there are still problems of this kind or that in today's China, and some western governments are still criticizing us in terms of our human rights condition and democracy, it is obvious to all that China is in the lead in the field of equality between sexes.

In our family we have also achieved equality between husband and wife.

One most important element in a family is that either of the husband or wife should be the decision maker and both should always consult each other before something is decided. It does not matter if the husband and wife do not agree with each on something for some time—just wait and see. There is always a way out, even if it is nothing but a compromise. However, Zhu Yanqun broke the rule in 1999 by spending 500000 yuan purchasing an apartment at the foot of the Huishan Mount for her parents without consulting me and getting my consent. She later explained to me that she did that out of the following two reasons: first, she well knew that I would never oppose to buy an apartment for my in-laws, and second, she would not care at all if I did disagree with her. This explanation of hers showed that she had already made up her mind to purchase an apartment for her parents, even at the cost of the rule between us that we must consult each other before any decision was made.

Zhu Yanqun and I got married in the eighties of last century when the country was still in the age of planned economy. As people's housing was all allotted to them by the institutions and companies they worked for, there were no such things in the market as commodity houses. We were living in a sixty-square-meter apartment which was barely spacious enough for the three of us. And it was obvious that it was not quite convenient for my parents or my wife's parents to stay with us. So for quite a long period we rented an apartment in the city for my in-laws who were from the countryside. Zhu Yanqun cannot bear to see and was reluctant to let her parents living in a rented house. So after we started our own business and set up a company and made some profits, she cannot wait any longer to buy an apartment for her parents.

It was reported that before someone was promoted in the local governments in some places, he or she would be investigated into whether they were good to their parents. Someone who is filial to his parents may not be a qualified public servant, but someone who is not good to his parents will definitely not be a good government official, for how can one serve the people well when he is bad to his own parents? In a similar way, how can a woman become a good wife when she is not a good daughter first of all? I deem it something important and good for my wife to buy her parents an apartment and therefore I had no objection at all as she had expected. On the contrary, not only did I have no dissent, instead I very much appreciated what she had done for her parents.

As the proverb says, spare the rod, spoil the child. Though it is not absolutely true, there is something in the saying. "Filial sons are from poor families." There might exist some interrelation between poverty and filial piety. My wife brought with her no dowry when we got married as she was from a poor family. But the daughter married is not the water splashed out. Instead she has given her parents much in return both materially and mentally. In this sense Zhu Yanqun is a woman who has achieved great promise.

## 报喜不报忧

报喜不报忧,是专制社会里下级对上级惯用的一种伎俩,因为上级的眼睛不是雪亮的,他官僚主义,你报喜不报忧,他就信以为真,他就认可你的政绩。至于忧,瞒不过有雪亮眼睛的老百姓,那不打紧,老百姓决定不了他这个"下级"的晋升和失意。民主社会则不然,你要选票,就得创造喜、消除忧,报喜不报忧不管用,你未报,喜忧已在人们的心中。新近笔者所住小区附近的一家菜场突然暂停营业,一问所以,省里来本市评比卫生城市也,不够卫生标准的菜场来不及整改,也懒得整改,一停,"忧"就不见了,不报忧是上策。

报喜不报忧是官场恶习,但用在家庭生活中成年的子女对年老的父母,不失为一种善意和良策。年龄大了,不仅身体每况愈下,心理承受也脆弱起来,经得起喜,却受不了忧了。老年人脱离了主流社会,解决各种人生难题的能力也少了许多,在此情况下,子女报忧就不明智,无助于自己解忧,却给长辈平添了忧,有弊而无利。

朱艳群深明对父母报喜不报忧的道理,且践行之。她既在新闻媒体工作,做事业单位的员工,又自己创办企业当总经理。她既要上厅堂,又要下厨房。工作和生活中的忧,她不比常人少,也许还多一点,但在父母面前,在公公婆婆面前,她总是每每表现得精神饱满,心情舒畅,用我妈——她婆婆的话说，她总是阳光灿烂。

朱艳群对父母不仅不主动报忧，还千方百计封锁有关忧的信息。2005年，《扬子晚报》登出一条消息，说省有关部门做出决定，要拆除本省高速公路沿线所有的高炮广告。这就意味着，我家广告公司的资产将不复存在，公司将破产。为了不让每天必看报的母亲看到这条坏消息，生出忧来，朱艳群早晨在家门口苦等送报人，没让当天的报纸进家门。还有一次，朱艳群心口有点不舒服，去医院一查，诊断为心肌炎，回家后母亲问起病情，她谎称感冒而已。有忧不报，有喜则必报。每当签到一笔较大的商业合同，每逢有税收优惠等政策利好，她都会喜形于色地在第一时间告之母亲。

新近在茶室喝茶，听到邻座一位中年男子在和同喝茶的一位女士说，他的儿子准备明年去美国留学，可家里经济上负担不起，为此他实在是忧，为了解忧，他反反复复在已双双离休的老父母面前报忧，终于让老人答应资助50万元供孙子出国之用。他这么说着，好像没什么歉意，倒是带了几分得意。而我在一旁听着，心里却有点不好受，并生出感慨：原来，子女向父母报忧，不仅是不懂事，还是图自身利益的。联系到妻的不报忧，更觉得她的可爱了。

## No Bad News but Good Ones

It was a frequently used trick in an autocratic society for the inferior officials to report to their superiors only what was good while concealing what is unpleasant. This was due to the fact that as bureaucratic as those top officials were, they always turned a blind eye to whatever his inferiors reported to him and accredited them with whatever they wrote in their reports. As for the bad news concealed, despite the fact that it would never escape the shrewd eyes of the public, the common people cannot do anything to affect either the promotion or the frustration of those low-rank officials. However, this will be a different story in a democratic society for if one expects to get votes from people, he has to create more pleasant information and wipe off the bad. It does not work if he holds back the bad news by only reporting the good one as whether he reports or not, both the pleasant and unpleasant information have already spread among people. Recently a market close to my residence community was temporarily suspended from business unexpectedly. I learned that as there was no time for the market to improve its hygienic condition before a provincial level inspection, it was just closed to avoid any trouble. It seems to be the best policy not to show the unpleasant situation to the inspectors.

This practice is definitely a vice popular in the officialdom, but can achieve good effects as a sound strategy if it is applied with good intentions in family life by adult sons and daughters to their old parents. With the advance of ages, old people not only are physically getting worse off but are mentally getting more and more fragile. They can bear the positive while they will also suffer from the negative. As the senior citizens stay away from the main stream social life, they become reduced in their abilities to handle various life problems. Under these circumstances, it is not wise for their grown-up children to tell them the bad news, for this neither helps to ease their worries nor does any good to their health.

Zhu Yanqun knows well the principle of concealing the unpleasant from her parents and so she well applies it in her daily life. She serves both as a media worker and the general manager of her own company, which means she has to take care of her work and business as well as our house chores. As a matter of fact, she has got no fewer troubles to handle in both work and life. However, she always appears before her parents and my parents a happy daughter full of spirit and energy. "She's always my sunshine," my mother once said.

Except that she never takes initiative to tell her parents those unpleasant information, Zhu Yanqun also tries her utter most to block bad news. The *Yangtze River Evening Post* carried a piece of news one day in 2005 that the government resolved to remove all the high-rise outdoor advertising alongside the expressways in the province. This meant that our advertising company's assets would no longer be in existence and the company was going bankrupt. In order to block the news from her mother who read newspaper every day, Zhu Yanqun waited for the postman at the door every morning to take the newspaper away. On another occasion Zhu Yanqun felt an ache in the chest and the doctor diagnosed that to be myocarditis. Upon return to home from the hospital, her mother asked about what was wrong and she lied that there was nothing serious but a cold. While concealing the bad information from her parents, she would always report to them whenever there is a piece of good news. For example, every time she signed a big contract or there is news about favorable policies like tax reduction, she would let her mother know as soon as possible.

Lately I overheard in a tea house a middle-aged man sitting at the next table telling a lady that his son was going to study in the United States the next year and that he was worried about the financial burden his family would take over. To solve the problem, he repeatedly mentioned his trouble to his retired parents and finally talked them into contributing 500000 yuan to cover the grandson's studying cost. His narration revealed no regret at all but only some complacency. I felt quite sorry for him on the side for I believe that it is not a sensible thing for sons and daughters to inform their parents of their own troubles, let alone to attempt to take advantage of the old people for their own interests. Thinking of what my wife does to her parents, I cannot help feeling how adorable she is.

# 听母亲说从前的事

《红楼梦》里的贾母，喜欢出谜面让子孙辈猜谜底。薛宝钗聪明，一听谜面，便知谜底。可她大智若愚，说老太太的谜太难猜，缠着要老太太自己说出谜底来，以此哄得老太太既得意又开心。

年少时读《红楼梦》，喜欢聪明而没有心计的林黛玉，对聪明而有心计的薛宝钗颇有几分贬义，总觉得她太功利、世故、不真，没有林黛玉可爱。人到中年再读《红楼梦》倒是给薛宝钗加了分，将她的世故看成了人情练达，将她的功利看成了人之常情，将她的猜出了谜底而装着猜不出的"不真"，看成了善意的谎言。不是吗？干吗要轻易说出谜底，扫了老太太的兴？让老太太开心才是硬道理，才是孝。

在母亲面前，朱艳群有时候活像薛宝钗。朱艳群的母亲长期在家做家庭妇女，对外面的主流社会知之甚少，因此年老以后在家中很少谈论时事，喜欢跟儿女辈孙子辈说说从前的事，尤其是她未嫁时娘家的事。这样的陈年老事，我这个女婿听了也不知有多少遍，可朱艳群总能不厌其烦地听，还时不时提一些小问题让母亲回答，以让母亲觉得，她饶有兴趣听那年那月的事。她母亲多次讲到200大洋的故事：朱艳群的外公有一年因家中失窃，弄得家无分文，为了200大洋，无奈之下把朱艳群的大姨妈嫁给了一个脑子有问题的男人，致使这个大姨妈吃了一辈子的苦，并使自己的一双儿女因遗传因素,智力异常低下。为了"讨好"母亲,朱艳群表态要我将此故事写成电影剧本,让母亲在有生之年看到这个故事变成电影。这下难为了我:隔行如隔山,我是有一点写作杂文的能力,可写作剧本不是我的所长,至今未能完成这个作业,好在女儿对创作剧本感兴趣,我把这个"皮球"踢给了她。

# Stories About the Past Told by Mum

Grandma Jia in *A Dream in Red Mansions* took delight in making her children and grand children guess riddles. Xue Baochai, her granddaughter, was smart enough to know the answer as soon as she heard of the riddles. However, she appeared to be slow-witted and kept on asking the old lady to reveal the answers. In this way she coaxed Grandma Jia to feel much pleased and happy with herself.

When I read the book many years ago as a teenager, I always liked Lin Daiyu, one of the heroines, much better as she was clever but without calculations, while another heroine, Xue Baochai was not as lovely as Lin because she was too material and sophisticatedly calculating, although she was no less clever than Lin Daiyu. This comment of mine toward Xue Baochai changed when I read the book again later as a middle-aged man, for now I regard her sophistication as her understanding of worldly wisdom and her desire for material gain as human nature. Isn't it the case that her pretense of not knowing the answers to the riddles is in certain ways some kind lies? Why should she speak out the answers readily to have the old lady's spirits dampened? It is the top priority to make the old lady happy.

Zhu Yanqun sometimes acted just like Xue Baochai toward her mother. Her mother, being a housewife for many years, knows very little about the mainstream society, and therefore she rarely talks about current affairs at home. Instead, she likes to tell her children and grandchildren things that happened in the past, in particular those before she got married. I have heard these old stories for numerous times, but Zhu Yanqun never gets bored and always listens to them with interest. From time to time she will raise some small questions to her mother so as to let her feel that the daughter is very interested in those stories. For many times her mother tells about the story of 200 silver dollars which goes like this: one year her grandfather's family suffered big loss by theft and to make 200 silver dollars to support the family, he cannot help but marry his elder daughter to a mentally retarded man. Zhu Yanqun's aunt suffered a great deal all her life and because of genetic factors, her son and daughter are all of abnormal low IQ. To "please" her mother, Zhu Yanqun declared that she would ask me to write a screen play based on the story and then turn it into a film for her mother. This really embarrassed me a lot as I am not good at writing play scripts at all though I can write essays in a way. The assignment has not been completed so far, but luckily my daughter takes some interest in writing scripts, and I readily passed the "rubber ball" to her.

# 乘飞机

从舒适的角度讲,有经验的人都知道,乘飞机不如坐火车、坐汽车,不如坐在家中的沙发里。可是没坐过飞机的人,总是希望体验一下坐上飞机飞上天的感受。诚如科幻作家刘慈欣所说:"这世界大多数人都想飞上天去,向尘世外瞥上一眼。"

在中国,70岁以上的老年人没乘过飞机的肯定是大多数。为了满足父母乘坐飞机的愿望,10年前朱艳群和父母从郑州返回无锡时,特意安排郑州至上海的航班。遗憾的是,这个航班开的是只有30多个座位的小型飞机,不仅机内设施简陋、陈旧,而且飞行时噪音大、不稳定。没坐过飞机的岳父母以为,飞机就是这个样,乘着还高兴着呢。

让父母坐这样差劲的飞机,朱艳群久久过意不去,不愿意让父母留下"飞机就是这个样"的印象,前年夏天,她丢下繁忙的公司事务,陪父母乘波音767飞了一趟海南。在崭新宽大的飞机上,朱艳群还拿出事先准备好的两条真丝围巾给一位空姐,让她以飞机上赠送的名义发给两位老人,让他们增添坐飞机的快乐。朱艳群的母亲常围着这条特殊的真丝围巾,好几次回忆坐飞机的快乐往事。

# Taking Flights

It is well-known among those experienced people that, for the sake of comfort, taking a flight is not as good as taking a train or coach bus, not even as good as sitting in the couch at home. However, those who never have the chance to take a flight will always expect to experience the feeling of flying into the sky. Just as what the science fiction writer Liu Cixin once said, "Most people in the world dream to fly into the sky and to take a glance at a world from outside the earth."

In China, the majority of old people over seventy have never got the opportunity to take a flight. Ten years ago when they were to return from Zhenzhou to Wuxi, Zhu Yanqun specially booked a flight from Zhenzhou to Shanghai so as to grant her parents' wish to fly. Unfortunately the flight, an ill-equipped small plane with only around thirty seats, was very noisy and bumping, which led the two first-time flight takers to think that plane were just like that and they were just as happy.

Zhu Yanqun was quite apologetic to let her parents take such an awful flight and she would not leave to them the impression that "airplane was just nothing but that". Then in the summer the year before last, she left behind her hectic company business to take a Boeing 767 flight to the Hainan Island. After boarding the spacious new plane, Zhu Yanqun took out two pre-prepared silk scarves and requested one airline stewardess to present them to her parents as a souvenir from the airliner. This definitely added to the two old people the joy of taking a flight. Later on Zhu Yanqun's mother would often put on that very special silk scarf and recall many times the happy experience to taking the flight.

# 说"乌托邦"

古今中外的实践表明，用"乌托邦"的思想去治理国家，人民必定遭殃。然而，在年老的父母面前说说与他们的生活息息相关的"乌托邦"，倒也无妨，倒也可以增加老年人的幸福指数。

朱艳群是给父母说"乌托邦"的能手。越是到了老年，人越是忧心寿命有限，来日不多，尤其是如今生活过得好，更怕好日子不长久。针对父母的这种心理，朱艳群有一次特意请来一位老中医给父母看身体，并让医生说，父母身体均十分健康，活过 100 岁不成问题。父母听此"乌托邦"，很是开心，增强了做百岁老人的信心。

朱艳群的母亲从小生活贫困，养成了节约的习惯，现在经济条件好了，还是舍不得花钱。她耳聋，需要配个助听器，可她一听说一个助听器价格要几千元，就执意不要。为了让她乐意接受，朱艳群又编"乌托邦"，说女儿花 2 元钱买彩票，中了一个奖，正好是助听器。老人居然信了。

因为长期做家庭妇女，没有退休工资，"低保"养活不了自己，几十年来只能靠儿女抚养，是母亲的心病。治此"病"，朱艳群还是用"乌托邦"，说政府规定，从 2011 年起，85 岁以上老年人享受每月 2000 元养老金。

朱艳群导演的一个又一个"乌托邦"，解了老人这样那样的忧，哄得父母开开心心。

# "Utopia"

The practice at all times and in all over the world has well shown that the people will be bound to suffer if a country is to be governed and managed with the idea of Utopia. However, it is quite alright and of no harm if we talk to the aged parents about the "Utopia" that is related to all aspects of their life. This may even increase old people's index of happiness.

Zhu Yanqun is well versed in describing such kind of "Utopia" to her parents. With the advance of ages, people are increasingly worried about their limited days left. Such worries would prevail particularly at present days for people are enjoying a much better life. In allusion to her parents' mentality of this kind, Zhu Yanqun once invited an old Chinese medicine doctor over to give them a medical check and asked the doctor before hand to tell her parents that they were both very fit and sound to live over a hundred years of age. Her parents were so joyful to hear about such "Utopia" comments to their health condition that they started to boost their confidence in living to be centenarians.

Zhu Yanqun's mother lived in poverty when she was a small child and therefore she has the habit of economizing on everything even though life is much better-off now. As she is losing her hearing day by day, it is obvious that she needs a hearing aid. But she insisted on not buying one when she was told that a hearing aid would cost several thousand yuan. Zhu Yanqun again had to fabricate a "Utopia" story that our daughter spent two yuan buying a lottery ticket and luckily won a prize which happened to be a hearing aid. To our surprise, her mother believed the story and readily agreed to wear the hearing aid.

Her mother has been troubled by one good anxiety to herself as that she has got no retire pension as a house wife and the basic subsistence provided by the government is far from suffice to support herself. To relieve her from such anxiety, once again Zhu Yanqun applied her therapy of "Utopia" story by telling her mother that old people over eighty-five years of age would enjoy an old-age pension of two thousand yuan a month from the government from the year 2011 on.

By working out such kind of "Utopia" stories, Zhu Yanqun has relieved many of her parents' worries to help them to live happily.

# 88 岁的观众

看电影的人叫观众。这些年,电影在中国似有复苏的趋势,观众多起来了,然观众中青年人居多,中年人不多,老年人更少,88 岁的观众几近于无。朱艳群的母亲今年 88 岁,在女儿的搀扶下进入电影院,吸引了好些人的眼球。

在西方社会,七八十岁的老年人别说进电影院,开跑车、开快车的也屡见不鲜。西方的老年人心态年轻,退休以后躲在家养老的少,他们会主动走进家外的社会。就是东方的日本老人也不同于中国的老人,他们哪怕进了养老院,也会走出去唱歌、喝酒、观影,甚至热衷于黄昏恋。中国人老了就像小小孩一样,生活的半径短得可怜,很少参加社会活动,结果是眼界窄了,活力少了,心情闷了,病也多了,老得快了,生活的乐趣微乎其微。

朱艳群不愿意自己的父母像左邻右舍的老年人一样过一种脱离"外面世界"的"闷"生活,她带着年老的父母出去旅游,进餐馆吃饭,到商场购物,去浴场洗澡,出入歌厅和影院。早些年父母花甲之年、古稀之年,在女儿的陪伴下出入公共场所并不起眼,近些年父母进入"奔九"高年,还在中青年的"天地"里出现,就成了例外和个案,引来的目光既有好奇的,也有羡慕的。

外面的世界真精彩!朱艳群说,创造条件让年老的父母常去外面世界"玩玩",有利于他们身心健康,也算是和国际社会接轨了。

# An Eighty-eight-year Old Movie-goer

People who go to see movies are called movie-goers. In recent years there is a trend in China that the film industry is reviving as there are more and more movie-goers. The majority of the movie-goers are young people. Not many middle-aged people and even fewer old people are among the movie-goers, while there are almost no sight of movie-goers who are at the age of eighty-eight. Zhu Yanqun's mother is eighty eight this year. One day she went to see a movie with the help of her daughter, which made quite a scene at the cinema.

It is said that people over seventy or eighty are often seen driving sports cars or even speeding in the western countries, let alone go to movie theatres. This might be because that they enjoy a young mentality and rarely stay at home to live out their life in retirement. They are only too glad to engage themselves with the social activities and the world away from home. In the east, even those aged Japanese people are quite different from their counterparts in China in that they would go out to sing, drink, go to movies or be high on late-life love even though they have been sent to old people's nursing home. The old people in China, however, are just like small children, with a very small life radius. They rarely get themselves engaged in social activities, and hence lack in vitality. Their aging process accelerates and health problems occur often. They then can enjoy very little fun and interest in their life.

Zhu Yanqun won't indulge her parents in taking a life similar to that of those old neighbors who are in low spirit and isolated from the outside world. So she often takes her parents to travel, dine in restaurants, do shopping as well as go to movie theatres and other places of entertainment. Earlier when they are in their sixties and seventies, it was not that conspicuous for them to go to different places with the company of their daughter. But now as they are close to ninety years of age and still appear in places that are usually patronized by the young and middle-aged people, they become some sort of unusual scene and have always attracted much attention with both curiosity and admiration.

The outside world is real splendid! Zhu Yanqun once said that it can be regarded as part of the international practice for people to create conditions for one's aged parents to go out to see the world. And this practice can do all the good to them, both physically and psychologically.

# 夸妈妈

朱艳群不兴无为而治,管理公司信奉有为而治,对员工比较严,很少表扬。可她对自己的妈妈,常常夸不离口。妈妈尚在中年的时候,她一般在背后夸妈妈的多,而当妈妈进入老年以后,她则喜欢当面夸妈妈。

朱艳群夸妈妈主要在几个方面,一是夸妈妈漂亮,气质好;二是夸妈妈知书达理,还写得一手好字;三是夸妈妈勤劳而节俭;四是夸妈妈美而不妖,不以姿色示人,正派,一门心思相夫教子。

朱艳群最欣赏妈妈常说的一句经典的话:"上等人自成人,中等人教成人,下等人教不成人。"她说,她从小立志自成人,很大程度上得益于这条语录。这条语录像传家宝一样,后来又传给了女儿。女儿告诉我,她三岁时听了这样的话,就对外婆表决心,长大以后不要不成人,也不要教成人,而要自成人。

夸别人,表扬别人,一般来说是有功用的,因为一则可以鼓励别人好上加好,二则可以拉近与被夸者、被表扬者的关系。俗话说,"好孩子都是表扬出来的",这也在说表扬的功能。朱艳群夸妈妈,一不追求妈妈再接再厉再进步,二没有讨好和拉关系的意思。朱艳群夸妈妈,除了由衷,就是让妈妈愉悦。朱艳群说,她深知:老年人是很在乎自己在子女心目中的形象的,你多夸夸他们,他们就更有自尊和自信,会少生出一些"人老珠黄不值钱"的感慨来。

# Complimenting Mum

Zhu Yanqun does not follow the doctrine of management by non-interference. She rarely gives compliments to her employees and is quite strict with them. However, to her mother, she is never mean in giving compliments. When her mother was in her middle ages, Yanqun more often complimented behind her. And when she gradually comes to her ripe years, Yanquan has started to give her compliments in person.

Zhu Yanqun's compliments to her mother mainly fall in several categories. Number one, compliments to her mother's beauty and disposition; number two, compliments to her being cultured and her handsome handwriting; number three, compliments to her diligence and thrift practice; number four, compliments to her decency and her devotion in assisting her husband and raising the children.

One classical saying often cited by her mother that Zhu Yanqun likes best is, a great person cultures himself into a great person, while an average person is raised to be an average one, and a cheap person is never taught to be a real one. She once said that, inspired to a great extent by this quotation, she had made up her mind to become a successful person ever since her childhood. Just like a family heirloom, this quotation has been passed on to my daughter. She told me that she once made her resolution before her grandmother to self-culture herself to be a great person when she grew up.

It is always effective to commend other people for, on the one hand, that will encourage people to do better, on the other hand, that will also draw close to the people who are praised. As the saying goes, good kids are all to be made out of compliments. This is another analysis of the function of compliments. However, what Zhu Yanqun does neither for the purpose of goading her mother to do better, nor for the intention of trying to establish a closer relationship with her. Her only intention with the heartfelt compliments is to delight her mother. She said that she knew quite clearly that old people really care about their impressions on their children. The more we praise them, the more self-esteem and confidence there will be nurtured in them, and therefore they will be less troubled by the feeling of becoming old and loose.

## 给妈读报

据统计，欧美国家的人看电视的少，看书读报的多，中国人反之，看电视的多，看书读报的少。在去往加拿大的飞机上，我还看到这样一个现象：西方人看纸质书的多，中国人玩电脑的多，当然其中也有的在电脑上读电子书。

电视和电脑是西方人发明的，纸质书是中国人发明的，没想到如今双方都不约而同地喜欢上对方的东西。这是一种文化现象，值得关注和研究，其背后，是隐含着民族素质的。

我们家的人，包括笔者、朱艳群、女儿高韵洌及朱艳群的妈，都是喜欢书报胜过喜欢电视和电脑的。我们有一个共同的作息，就是吃过晚饭先"饭后百步"——散步，再回到客厅各自阅览书报。几年前，朱艳群的妈还能戴着老花镜看报，近几年，视力更差了，要用放大镜才能看清楚。用放大镜看，阅读的速度慢了许多，为了让母亲看得轻松些、多一些，朱艳群常常为妈妈读报，一读就是个把小时。

我发现，朱艳群为妈读报，还蛮讲究内容选择的，四个方面的信息读得比较多。一是时事新闻，二是风景名胜介绍，三是社会新鲜事，四是生活小常识。朱艳群向我给出了选择上述内容的理由：她妈虽没高学历，但满身知识分子气息，关心社会事务是知识分子的特质，所以她要读时事新闻。她妈已到高龄,到处旅游已不现实,所以"听听"风景名胜,也算到此一游。老人如小孩,喜欢新鲜事,所以给她报"鲜"料。老人大事不做了,生活小常识正好适用,所以给她"读读"。

在一对布料沙发上,端坐的女儿手捧报纸细声慢读,斜靠的妈妈洗耳恭听,一幅贵族的生活画。我用相机留下了如此的美妙。

# Reading Newspaper to Mum

Statistics show that in Europe and American countries there are more people reading newspapers and books than watching TV, while it is just the opposite among Chinese people. I also noticed in my flight to Canada that more western people were reading books while more Chinese people were playing with computers. Of course among them some may be reading ebooks on screen.

TV and computer are both invented by westerners while printed books are invented by Chinese people. It happens to coincide that these days they fall to favor the other side's inventions. As a cultural phenomenon, it is worth further study as there exists certain implications of national quality somewhere behind.

My family members like Zhu Yanqun, my daughter Gao Yunlie, my mother-in-law and myself all prefer reading than watching TV and using computers. We have one habit in common, that is, we all like to take a walk after dinner and then return home to read newspapers and magazines of each other's own likings in the sitting room. A couple of years ago, Zhu Yanqun's mother was able to read newspapers by her own with the help of reading glasses. In recent years, however, as her eyesight is deteriorating, she has to read with a magnifier, which means she reads much slowly now. In order to help her mother read more relaxingly for more information, Zhu Yanqun frequently reads newspaper to her, usually for over one hour each time.

I have noticed that Zhun Yanqun is quite meticulous in selecting the contents that she reads to her mother. Mostly the information and news fall in four types, respectively, the current affairs news, articles about scenic spots, social novelties, and life tips and facts. She explained to me once why she chose to read those stuff. She reads the current affairs news to her as her mother is a person of intellectual nature though she has never received higher education. Her mother is unlikely to travel around in her advanced years, thus "listening to" the introduction about those scenic spots may be well considered a form of imaginary tour. And as old people are in many ways much alike small children, they like to know about those news and interesting things. Last but not least, because old people are not able to do those major house chores, it is only too appropriate to "read her" some of the life tips and facts.

And there is often seen an aristocratic life scene in my house: sitting in a separate cloth-covered sofa, the daughter reads a newspaper in a soft and rhythmical voice, while the mother listens attentively with a joyful look on face. I cannot help but record such wonderful moments with my camera from time to time.

# 双重标准

双重标准的名声好像不太好,中国政府老是批评美国政府在民主和人权问题上搞双重标准。

记得鲁迅先生也搞过双重标准,他在公开场合提倡白话文,却私下里买文言文的书给母亲,给母亲写信写的也是文言文。显然,鲁迅的母亲是看得懂白话文的,鲁迅给她写信用文言文,并非交流的需要,而是照顾到母亲的习惯和喜好。鲁迅提倡白话文,这是对中国大众的,不包括自己的母亲,母亲不是他教育的对象,母亲只是他孝敬的对象,所以适合母亲的,就是鲁迅对母亲的标准。

我觉得鲁迅的双重标准,不仅不自私、不不公平、不可恶,是可以接受的,甚至是可贵的。是一种原则性和灵活性的统一,是既有原则又有人情味的,值得提倡。

朱艳群也有自己的双重标准。她严以待己,也严以待人,却宽以待母。朱艳群对别人的严,试举一例:她唯一的宝贝女儿3岁时不小心走路摔痛而哭,她不仅不安慰之,反而严厉批评女儿不该走路不看路,并要求她自己站起来,不许再哭。而对她的母亲,她是从不批评的,别人宠独生子女,宠宠物,她宠妈,哪怕妈说错了什么,做错了什么,她也从不责怪。她说,老人就像瓷器,易碎,得用心保护。笔者烧饭烧焦了,朱艳群会有非议,她母亲每每煮稀饭不是烧熟而是焐烂,煮出来的稀饭很难吃,我要指点一二,朱艳群也不允,生怕老人"见气"。朱艳群的母亲有时和家里的保姆产生小矛盾,她就不分青红皂白护着母亲,宁愿背后向保姆道歉。

对朱艳群严待包括自己在内所有人却宽以待母的双重标准,我起先有点看不惯,随着岳父母的渐渐老去,我理解了朱艳群,且对她产生了敬意!

# Double Standard

The adoption of double standard seems to be an ill-named practice. The Chinese government often criticizes the American government for its practice of double standard in areas of democracy and human rights issues.

I remember that Mr. Lu Xun, the great thinker and writer, also practiced double standard. In public he advocated the adoption of writings in the vernacular, while in private he bought for her mother books written in classical Chinese and wrote to her mother in the same style. Apparently Lu Xun's mother can read writings in vernacular. He wrote to her in classical Chinese for the sake of her mother's habit and preferences instead of the need for communication. Lu Xun's support to the use of vernacular in writing was a standard for the general public in China and was not for his mother because she was the one he treated with filial respect but not the one he educated. In this sense, what was appropriate to his mother was Lu Xun's standard towards her.

I therefore find that Lu Xun's double standard is not only unselfish, fair, and acceptable but also commendable, for it is the combination of principle and flexibility with a touch of human kindness, which deserves recommendation.

Zhu Yanqun practices her own double standard. She is strict both with herself and other people, but is very lenient with her mother. Here is an example to illustrate her strictness toward people. Once her three-year-old only daughter lost her balance and fell to the ground. Because of the hurt, she cried bitterly. Instead of comforting her, Zhu Yanqun scolded her for not walking carefully and asked her to stand up by herself and stop crying. Yet she never blames her mother for anything. Other people would spoil their only child or pet their pets, but she usually dotes on her mother even her mother has said something or done something wrong. She says that old people are just like fragile porcelain that needs meticulous care. She would always complain if I burned the rice. But she would never allow me to speak up whenever her mother cooked unpalatable porridge from time to time lest that she took offence and got angry. Occasionally, Zhu Yanqun's mother would get into troubles with our house maid. And when that happened, Zhu Yanqun would indiscriminately stand for her mother and then apologize to the maid later behind her mother's back.

At first I was not used to Zhu Yanqun's double standard of being strict with everyone including herself but lenient to her mother. By and by, as my in-laws grow old, I gradually begin to understand Zhu Yanqun's practice and give her my respects for that.

# 瓜子和胡桃

　　瓜子和胡桃是普通而美味的小吃,男女老少都喜食之。瓜子和胡桃还有一个共同点:有壳,剥了壳才能吃。剥壳有点麻烦,可唯其麻烦,才得之不易,才不会大口大口地吃。得之不易之物似乎更有价值,大口大口地多吃就少滋味,少吃就多滋味。所以,从店里买来的已经剥好了的瓜子肉和胡桃肉,总觉得不如自己剥壳的味道好。

　　据动物学家观察,乌鸦也喜欢吃胡桃肉。当然,乌鸦自己是没能力剥开胡桃壳的。不过乌鸦智商奇高,它们有借人类敲碎胡桃壳的办法:它们衔着一颗胡桃在路边等待,直到交通信号灯由绿变红,便飞下来,将坚果丢在汽车车轮前,然后飞走。当绿灯再次亮起,它们再飞回来捡食那些被车轮碾碎外壳的胡桃。

　　朱艳群对我说,小时候和哥哥姐姐们围坐在妈妈身边,吃着由妈妈亲手剥开的瓜子肉和用小榔头敲碎壳的胡桃肉,是一种幸福。出于对母亲的感激和报恩,参加工作有了收入以后,朱艳群常常会买一些瓜子和胡桃,如同当年吃母亲剥开的瓜子肉和胡桃肉一样,也亲手剥瓜子和胡桃给母亲吃。尽管现在有了现成的瓜子肉和胡桃肉供应,她还是乐于劳作一番,以此体现对母亲的反哺。

# Sunflower Seeds and Walnuts

Sunflower seeds and walnuts are ordinary but delicious snacks loved by all people regardless of age and sex. Sunflower seeds and walnuts have another thing in common: with shell, the shells must be removed before they can be eaten. Shelling is inconvenient, but it's the inconvenience that makes us cherish the kernels inside, so we won't gobble them down. Hard-earned stuff seems to be of more value. So if we gobble, it tastes not so delicious, but if we eat little, it tastes better. So, in terms of tastes, shelled sunflower seeds and walnut kernels bought from stores always seem inferior to those shelled by ourselves.

As is observed by zoologists, crows favor walnut kernels, too. Of course, crows are incapable of cracking the nuts. But crows are peculiarly intelligent and have their unique way of cracking nuts by taking advantage of human beings. A crow would hold a walnut in its beak and wait by the roadside. When the traffic light turns from green to red, it will dive down, throwing the nut in the front of car wheels and then fly away. When the green light goes on again, they will fly back to pick up and eat the walnuts whose shells have been crushed by wheels.

Zhu Yanqun used to tell me that in her childhood, it was great enjoyment sitting with brothers and sisters around their mother and eating sunflower seed shelled with hands by their mother and walnut kernels cracked with a small hammer by their mother. Out of gratitude to her mother, after she had a job and got paid, Zhu Yanqn often buys some sunflower seeds and walnuts. She is now shelling by hand sunflower seeds and walnuts for her mother, exactly the way her mother did for her in the past years. Even though there are ready-to-eat sunflower seeds and walnut kernels for sale, she is still willing to labor a bit so as to show her regurgitation-feeding for her mother.

## 带妈上班

我在加拿大温哥华发现一个现象：西方人比中国人好动也能静。我在海边的一幢房子里住过一段时间。见堤岸上凡是跑步的，几乎都是西方人；凡是散步的，百分之百是中国人。这是西方人比中国人好动的例子。西方人比中国人能静的例子是，住在人烟稀少、深山老林的都是西方人，中国人耐不得住在"鸟鸣山更静"、放眼不见人的地方。

人类是群居动物，中国人尤甚。我有一个当公务员的同学，在谈到理想的老年生活时说，老年人怕寂寞，最适合居住和生活的地方是美国的拉斯维加斯，那里许多的老年人和年轻人一样，可以长时间泡在繁华和热闹的各式大酒店玩乐，无需"耐得寂寞"。朱艳群怕母亲在家清静得无聊，常常带着她上班。公司里年轻人多，热闹，遂了老人的心。懂礼貌的员工叫她"外婆"的有之，帮她泡茶添水的有之，听她说说"老话"的有之，一切的一切，都让她愉悦。公司里组织的春游和秋游，朱艳群也将母亲视作"员工"，列入"名单"。

退休在家享清福是一种福，人老了还和众多年轻人一起生活游乐，也是一种福。合久必分，分久必合，是一种规律。动久想静，静久想动，也是一种规律。让母亲动动静静，静静动动，是朱艳群照顾老人晚年生活的一种原则和方法。

# Taking Mum to Work

I noticed a phenomenon in Vancouver, Canada. That is, the westerners are sportier than the Chinese but they are more capable of living a peaceful life than the Chinese. I used to live in a house near the sea for some time. As I saw, almost all those who jogged on the embankment were the westerners; and those who walk were 100% the Chinese. This example clearly shows that the westerners are sportier than the Chinese. An example to show the westerners are more peaceful is that people who live in sparsely-populated mountainous areas are all the westerners. The Chinese can't bear to live in untraversed places where "bird singing has made the mountain seem more peaceful".

Human beings like to live in groups, the Chinese in particular. When talking about the ideal life of old age, a former classmate of mine who is currently a government employee said that the elderly fear loneliness, so the ideal settling place for them is Las Vegas in the States. There many old people can spend long time having fun in the bustling and busy hotels like the young people, without "bearing loneliness". Worrying that her mother will be bored of staying idle at home, Zhu Yanqun often takes her to work. There are many young people in the company whose liveliness is what her mother prefers. Among the polite employees, some call her "grandma", some serve tea and top up the cup, and some enjoy listening to her "old story". All these she enjoys to her heart's content. Even in spring and autumn outings, Zhu Yanqun will put her mother's name in the list of "employees".

It's enjoyment to retire and lead a peaceful life. It's another kind of enjoyment for the old people to live a hilarious life with a lot of young people. It's a universal rule that division occurs after prolonged unification and unification occurs after prolonged division. It's another rule that people need peace after prolonged animation and animation after prolonged peace. So it's Zhu Yanqun's principle and method of taking care of the old people's life to make her mother live a life where peace and animation occur alternately.

# 帮妈找"伴"

这里的"伴",不是伴侣的意思,朱艳群的父亲还健在,和母亲的感情也尚可,女儿无需替妈做红娘找"老伴"。这里的"伴",还丰富着呢!朱艳群和我都长期在江苏人民广播电台工作,对广播有感情,觉得收音机该是陪妈的好"伴",于是替她买了高档的收音机,又备足了电池,并指导她江苏新闻广播、无锡新闻台等的频率是什么。

除了"播伴",朱艳群还为母亲订了五种报纸,称为"报伴";还常常为母亲选购书籍,称为"书伴";还为母亲买了一个琴,称为"琴伴"。

我有一个文友一次和我一起春游,见到满目的山山水水、花花草草,感慨地说,风景虽美,总不如美女好看啊!借用他的句式,"播伴"、"报伴"、"书伴"、"琴伴"虽好,总不如"友伴"啊!朱艳群的父母长期居住在农村小镇,来城里以后,特别是到了晚年,昔日的"友伴""走"的走了,散的散了,到了新的环境,多有无友的苦处。为了解决这个问题,朱艳群在我们居住的小区,满院子找适合和她妈交友的人选。功夫不负有心人,终于找到了一个年龄相仿、学识相当、价值观趋同的老奶奶,巧的是,这位老奶奶说的还是朱艳群老家的方言。这下好了,"两老"见面常常"千句少"。

"伴",是老年人的精神需求,在物质生活日益丰富的今天,"伴"的意义显得尤为重要。

# Looking for "Partners" for Mum

The "partner" here does not refer to spouse. Zhu Yanqun's father is still alive and quite compatible with her mother, so there is no need for their daughter to serve as a match-maker and look for a "partner" for the mother. The "partner" mentioned here is actually versatile! Zhu Yanqun and I had been working in Jiangsu People's Radio for a long time and are really attached to radio. We found the radio a good "partner" for her mother, so we bought for her an expensive one, loaded it with batteries and taught her how to tune to Jiangsu News Broadcasting, Wuxi News and so on.

In addition to the "radio partner", Zhu Yanqun also subscribed to five newspaper for her mother, which are so-called "newspaper partners", often bought books for her mother, thus called "book partner" and bought a piano for her, which is her "piano partner".

I used to travel with a literary friend in spring. Seeing the beautiful landscape that greeted the eyes, he commented with sentiment that beautiful as the landscape was, it paled beside beauties. In his sentence pattern, "broadcasting partners", "newspaper partners", "book partners" and "piano partners" are good but still inferior to "friend partners"! Zhu Yanqun's parents had been all along living in rural areas. Since they settled in the city, especially at their old ages, some of the former "friend partners" have passed away and some got separated. In the new environment, most of these elderly people are annoyed with absence of close friends. To settle the problem, Zhu Yanqun spared no efforts to look for the candidates compatible to her mother as friends in our neighborhood. Her efforts have paid off. She ended up finding such an elderly lady who was of the similar age, with comparable knowledge and experience and similar values. Coincidentally, the lady spoke a dialect that belongs to Zhu Yanqun's hometown. So it's not hard to imagine when these "two elderly ladies" meet, "a thousand words" are far too few for them.

The "partner" is the spiritual demand of the elderly. In today's society where the material life gets increasingly richer, the "partner" is of particularly great significance.

# 写毛笔字画画

毛泽东说:"与天斗,其乐无穷;与地斗,其乐无穷;与人斗,其乐无穷。"我说,人生在世,要玩得好,就要跟自然玩——游山玩水,跟人玩——与人交流,跟自己玩——自找乐趣。

为了让进入老年的母亲自找乐趣——跟自己玩,朱艳群诱惑她重拾年轻时的所长和爱好——写毛笔字、画画。写毛笔字、画画,说干就干,朱艳群很快替母亲买来了毛笔字帖和画画的纸笔。每天一下班,朱艳群就组织我和女儿进母亲的"书房"观字赏画。

说实话,她母亲虽谈不上书艺高超,画技惊人,字倒也写得端庄标致,画画得颇有灵气。观赏还不够,朱艳群还提议我们一家三口照着她母亲写的字写字,按着她母亲画的画画画,然后由老人为我们评分。结果是:女儿字写得最好,朱艳群画画得最好,而我写的字、画的画都是末等的。这也正常,我小时候特别调皮,没心思干写字、画画之类的"耐心事",如今拿不出手,正应了那句话:"少壮不努力,老大徒伤悲。"见我因落后不好意思,善解人意的岳母马上替我解围,说,人各有所长,要是比写文章,高鸣还是可以的。

据说马克思的夫人燕妮晚年写小说,大有成就。蒋介石的第一夫人宋美龄晚年作画,一百岁高龄还在美国办画展,大获好评。想来这两位名女人晚年的作为不是企图成名成家吧,大约也是跟自己玩玩的意思而已。

# Brush Writing and Painting

Mao Zedong has put it, "There is endless enjoyment in fighting against the heavens, the earth and the human beings." I would say that if you want to live an enjoyable life and have fun, you'd better play with nature— doing sightseeing among hills and rivers, play with people— communicating with people, and play with yourselves— looking for fun by yourselves.

To make her elderly mother have fun and enjoy herself, Zhu Yanqun has tempted her to resume her old hobbies in the youth— brush writing and painting. With the thought in her mind, she started right now, buying copybooks for calligraphy and paper and brush-pencil for painting. Every day after work, Zhu Yanqun got our daughter and me to view and admire the calligraphy and paintings in her mother's "study".

To be honest, although her mother's works are far from superb, the characters were written in a neat and beautiful way and paintings were painted with vividness. Besides viewing, Zhu Yanqun even suggested that we three copy characters from her mother's calligraphy and copy the paintings from her mother's originals and her mother would serve as the judge to grade our works. The result is, my daughter does best in calligraphy, Zhu Yanqun does best in painting, and both my calligraphy and paintings are ranked at bottom. It's quite understandable. I used to be very naughty in my childhood and had no patience for such "stuff" as writing characters and painting. Now the works turn out to be unpresentable, which is the very portrayal of the saying "A lazy youth, a lousy age". Seeing me embarrassed at falling behind, my understanding mother-in-law saved me from embarrassment by saying that each one has his strength and Gao Ming does quite well in writing.

It's said Jenny, Karl Marx's wife, made great achievements in writing novels in her old age. Song Meiling, first lady of Jiang Jieshi, painted at her old age. She held a painting exhibition in the States at the age of 100 and has won great acclaim. It seems to me that the two female celebrities did so at the old age probably not for personal fame or career, but for fun only.

## 学英语

　　学习使人进步。朱艳群大概还懂得学习使人快乐,学了以后的进步也使人快乐的道理,她居然鼓励当年已 76 岁高龄的母亲学习英语,说你外孙女在国外学英语的,以后回国你们一老一少偶尔说几句英语也是一大快事。

　　我开始反对朱艳群让她母亲学英语,理由是学英语很苦的,况且她年龄这么大了,哪能记得住那些单词和语法。朱艳群说:毛泽东不也是建国以后、老年学的英语吗?我说:毛泽东那么好学,而且学外语时不过六十来岁,你妈怎么行?没想到朱艳群她妈还真行,不仅有兴趣学,而且学起来进步不慢,不久,26 个字母倒背如流,你好、再见、晚安、今天、明天、可以、多少钱等英语说法会而不忘。看到自己尚有学习能力,老人异常开心。我试想,这开心里面,还有庆幸自己"不算太老"的成分吧。

　　今年春节,女儿考考外婆以前学过的英语单词遗忘了没有,不料外婆一词不差,问其故,答曰:我年龄大了,所以学得不多,但已学的那些,我是"学而时习之"的,也叫做"笨鸟多飞"吧。

　　"六十岁学打拳",是形容学得不是时候了,其实"八十岁学打拳"为时也不晚。看来,朱艳群让母亲学英语,没错。

# Learning English

Learning leads to progress. Probably Zhu Yanqun also knows that learning and progress that ensues both lead to happiness. She encouraged her then 76-year-old mother to learn English, convincing her that since her granddaughter was learning English abroad, sometimes it would be a delightful event for both of them to have short conversations in simple English.

At the beginning, I was against this on the ground that learning English is really painstaking and given her old age, how she could possibly memorize those words and grammar rules. Zhu Yanqun defended herself by noting that Mao Zedong also didn't start learning English until after the foundation of our nation, at an old age. I refuted that Mao Zedong was really fond of learning and was only in his sixties when he was learning English, and how her mother could possibly make it. To my surprise, Zhu Yanqun's mother did make it. She not only was interested but also progressed quite quickly. Before long, she was able to recite the English alphabet backwards fluently and quite well versed in such English expressions as hi, good bye, good night, today, tomorrow, ok, how much and so on. Seeing that she herself still has learning capacity, the elderly lady was extremely pleased. I assume that in her pleasure elements of felicitating herself that "she was not too old to learn" could be involved.

This Spring Festival, my daughter tested her grandmother to check whether she had forgotten the English words previously learned. To her surprise, her grandmother made no mistake on a single word. When asked about the reason, she replied that she was too old to learn much, but she "learned and constantly reviewed" what she had learned, so she was actually "a slow sparrow flying more".

"Learning boxing at sixty" depicts people who don't learn at the right time. In fact, it's even not late to "learn boxing at eighty". It turns out exactly correct that Zhu Yanqun has encouraged her mother to learn English.

## 让母亲当"文秘"

朱艳群的母亲一生中为家庭做出了重要贡献,不仅含辛茹苦养育了四个子女,还帮着儿子带孙子,帮着女儿带外孙女。老年以后,总怕自己没有了价值,成为子女的拖累。

为了打消母亲的上述"多虑",朱艳群跟我商量,要我把写了草稿准备向全国各地发的文章,让她妈誊写成"定稿"。当年我几乎天天动笔写一篇千字议论文,发往各地各类报章杂志。每天完成千字的抄写工作,并装进信封投进附近的邮局,工作量不算太大,60多岁的老人正好适合。我因为"熟能生巧",稿件发表率接近百分之百,以平均每篇8元稿费计,月收入倒也有200多元。这在上世纪80年代初已是一笔不小的数字,相当于我当记者月工资的一倍。朱艳群把其中的一半分给她母亲,又等同于她母亲每月拿到一份不低的工资。每当收到稿费单,岳母既为我文章的发表高兴,又为创造了收入快乐。尽管岳母知道这"创造"的首功是我,但她也毕竟付出了劳动,体现了自己的剩余价值。

上世纪90年代以后,随着市场经济的深化,文章不值钱了,看文章的人少了,我们暂停了以文创收,开始了以商创收。为了继续让母亲老有所为,实现价值,朱艳群安排母亲当自办企业的"文秘",专职保管商业合同。考虑到母亲已70多岁,怕其记性差,犯糊涂出差错,实际让她保管的是特意制作的假合同。新近一检查,上百份"合同"理得井井有条,分门别类,便于查阅。现在想想,要是当年让她管理真的合同,倒也无妨。

在《精养女儿》的书中,我曾说过,小孩的"小",往往是被我们看小的,其实没那么小。在这里我要说,老人的"老",同样往往是被我们看老的,其实没那么老。让老人当"文秘",可以让老人降低心理年龄,增加幸福感。

# Hiring Mum as The "Secretary"

Zhu Yanqun's mother has made significant contributions to the family in her lifetime. She bore bitter hardships bringing up four children, and also helped her children rear the next generation. In the old age, she is always worried about being worthless and posing a burden to her children.

To dismiss her mother's above-mentioned "apprehension", Zhu Yanqun consulted with me and suggested that after I finished my drafts to be contributed to the nationwide editorial offices, I should leave the work of copying drafts to her mother to finalize. At that time, I wrote a piece of argumentative writing of around one thousand words almost every day and submitted it to all kinds of magazines and newspapers nationwide. It doesn't count as a heavy workload for a lady in her sixties to copy around one thousand characters, put the script into an envelope and then drop it into the nearby post office every day. It's actually quite acceptable for her. Owing to the rule of "practice makes perfect", I got almost all articles submitted published. If calculated at the rate of eight yuan per article, my monthly publications may bring me an income of more than 200 yuan. In the early 1980s, it was quite a fortune, and was almost twice my monthly income of being a journalist. Zhu Yanqun then spared half of it to pay her mother, which was like her mother earned a decent income every month. Every time

I received the notice of payment for my published articles, my mother-in-law was delightful because of publication of my articles and also creation of her own income. Although she knew the "creation" was primarily owed to me, after all, she had also made contributions and realized her own value.

Since the 1990s, with the deepening of market economy, articles became worthless and the number of readers declined. We stopped generating income by writing and started generating income with business. To make her mother always engaged in something and realize the self-value, Zhu Yanqun arranged for her mother to serve as "secretary" of our own company by putting commercial contracts under her custody. Assuming that she was in her seventies and might commit mistakes for her declining memory, we left to her contracts faked deliberately. In a recent inspection, hundreds of "contracts" were arranged under categories and in good order for the sake of convenience. Now we admit there was definitely no harm if we had let her manage the genuine one.

In the book of *Daughte-rearing:A Chinese Family's Way*, I used to say that young kids appear "young" because we mistook them as being young. They are actually not that young. Here I would like to point out that the old appear "old" also because we mistak them as being old. They are actually not that old. Hiring the elderly as "secretaries" can help them feel psychologically younger and spiritually happier.

# 生日感言

朱艳群对自己的生日,对我的生日,对女儿的生日,并不怎么放在心上,而对父母亲的生日,她是重视的,总要为他们办一桌,把哥哥姐姐等亲人邀来,共祝老人生日快乐。

每当母亲过生日,朱艳群还会特别安排一个节目:请母亲发表"生日感言"。让小辈们聆听母亲的教诲。

有人说,人有两大欲望,一是把别人口袋里的钱挣过来,一是把自己的思想装到别人的脑子里去。朱艳群说,母亲老了,已然没有了挣钱的欲望,但把自己的想法传播出去,尤其是传给子女的心念还是有的。让母亲借发表"生日感言"的机会,说说自己的人生经验,对听众是一种得益,对说者也是一种快乐。

每年听岳母的"生日感言",总有一种胜读书的感觉。这里不妨说说印象最深的几句话。岳母说,做人就要学老子,低调、示弱,如水一样温柔而谦卑,这样就可以包容一大片,被别人所接受。做事就要学孔子,有责任,有担当,有作为。生活就要学庄子,轻松潇洒,天真快乐。遇挫折、遭磨难,就要学佛家,想得开,放得下,不患得,不患失。讲理就得学墨子,讲兼爱,讲大众听得进去的话,如马克思的"全世界无产者联合起来",孙中山的"天下为公",毛泽东的"为人民服务"、"向雷锋同志学习"。

"不听老人言,吃亏在眼前。"此话未必正确,因为老人言也是有对有错的,一概听之,难免犯错。而朱艳群母亲上述的几句老人言,思来想去倒蛮有哲理,似乎可以听听。

# Birthday Speech

Zhu Yanqun does not take her own birthday, my birthday and our daughter's birthday seriously. But she does attach great importance to her parents' birthdays. To celebrate it, she usually holds a banquet and invites her brothers, sisters and other relatives to come over.

Every time her mother celebrates her birthday, Zhu Yanqun will arrange a special program, that is, inviting her mother to deliver a "birthday speech", from which the younger generations could get her earnest teachings.

It's said that people have two desires. One is to earn money from others' pockets, and the other is to put their own thoughts into others' minds. Zhu Yanqun said that her mother was old and had lost interest in making money, but she still had the desire to disseminate her own ideas to the young generations. So it would bring benefits to the audience and meanwhile happiness to the speaker to let her mother talk on her own life experience in the form of "birthday speech".

Every year, listening to my mother-in-law's "birthday speech" makes me feel I benefit from it more than from reading. Here I may as well talk about the most impressive quotes of hers. According to her, in terms of personal conduct, people must learn from Laozi and try to keep low-key, not aggressive and as gentle and humble as water. In this way, we can tolerate more and get accepted by others. In terms of dealing with affairs, people must learn from Confucius and try to be conscientious, responsible and capable. In terms of life attitudes, people must learn from Zhuangzi and try to be natural and unrestrained, innocent and happy. In the face of setbacks and hardship, people must learn from Buddhism, always looking on the bright side of things and being resilient and resolute, without worrying about personal gains and losses. In terms of doing ideological work, people should learn from Mozi and try to practice universal love, by using words that appeal to ordinary people, such as "proletarians of the world unite" by Marx, "the whole world as one community" by Sun Yat-sen, "serve the people" and "learn from Comrade Lei Feng" by Mao Zedong.

As a saying goes, "if you don't follow the old people's words, you might suffer losses soon." The statement is not necessarily correct, because words uttered by the old could be wrong. If we follow all, we might well commit mistakes. But there seems to be wisdom in the words uttered by Zhu Yanqun's mother, one of the old people, and there is no harm in following them.

# 首月工资

上世纪 70 年代进入工厂的人都知道,学徒期月工资都是十几元。我被分配在钢铁厂,重工业企业,工资高一点,每月 15 元。朱艳群在印刷厂,轻工业企业,工资低一点,每月 13 元。

首月工资怎么处理?我父母亲当年属于高收入人群,不需我上交工资,我跟奶奶感情好,便把工资的一半孝敬奶奶,一给就是多年,直到 8 年后奶奶去世。和朱艳群恋爱以后,我曾问过她如何支配首月工资的。她告诉我,她是花 7 元钱买了绒线,替母亲织了一件毛衣。她说,母亲节约,要是直接交钱,母亲不会给自己买衣服,只会"取之于子女,用之于子女",或干脆帮子女存着,日后一并奉还。

我原先想,对父母好,只是一个态度问题,听了朱艳群买绒线帮母亲织毛衣的故事,我方觉,对父母好,也有一个方法问题呢。

说到朱艳群对母亲好的方法,我想起了另外一件有关衣服的事。2001 年冬,朱艳群和我陪她妈去商场买了一件老人的大衣,当时穿着好像还挺合身的,可回家半月后再穿发现太紧了些。朱艳群的妈妈让女儿去商场换一件大一些的,不料去换时原先那个摊位已变了品牌和经营者。怎么办呢?倘若如实将情况告知母亲,老人肯定会舍不得花了冤枉钱的。于是,朱艳群一方面将那件大衣送给了朋友的母亲,一方面对母亲说,没换成大一号的,但退货成功。这个谜,她母亲至今未解。

# Salary of The First Month

People who started working in factories in the 1970s all know that salary for people of apprenticeship was only a little more than ten yuan. I was assigned a position of working in a steel plant. It's an enterprise of heavy industry, so I was entitled to a higher salary of fifteen yuan per month. Zhu Yanqun worked in a printing house which was an enterprise of light industry, so her salary was lower, being thirteen yuan per month.

How to deal with the salary for the first month then? In those days, my parents belonged to the high income group. Therefore, there was no need for me to turn in my salary. And I was so closely attached to my grandma that I gave away half of my earnings to her to show my respect and love. Such a practice had been going on for a couple of years till my grandma passed away eight years later. After I dated with Zhu Yanqun, I asked her how she dealt with her salary of the first month. She told me that she had spent seven Yuan buying knitting wool and knit a sweater for her mother. She further explained that since her mother was thrifty, if she just turned in money, her mother wouldn't buy herself clothes with the money, but "benefit people with what's obtained from them"; or her mother would simply put the money aside for her children and return all the savings to them in due time.

It was my original thought that treating parents well was merely an issue of attitude. It was not until I heard Zhu Yanqun's story of buying knitting wool and knitting a sweater for her mother that I realized treating parents also involves diplomacy.

Zhu Yanqun's way of treating her mother well just reminds me of another thing relevant to clothes. In the winter of 2001, Zhu Yanqun and I accompanied her mother to the department store to buy a coat for the elderly. It seemed to fit her well in the store, but after we took it home, half a month later, it turned out to be a bit too tight. Zhu Yanqun's mother let her go to the store to swap for a larger size. However, when she got there, she found the previous stall was under new name and new ownership. What to do then? If told the truth, her mother would surely regret having spent the undeserved money. Then Zhu Yanqun gave away the coat to her friend's mother, but told her mother she had failed to swap for a larger size but had managed to get a refund. Her mother has been kept in the dark on this till now.

# 朱艳群洗头

除了理发店的洗头工,朱艳群比一般的人洗头多,她不仅勤洗自己的头,还常为我洗头,常为她母亲洗头,常为小时候的女儿洗头。

朱艳群为自己洗头多有三个原因。一是她特讲究个人卫生。二是她节约,以此省了去理发店洗头的钱。三是她独创了只有自己会"盘"的发型,几十年不变,理发师做不来。

朱艳群为我洗头的原因是,我时常忽略洗头的事,无论是自己洗,还是去理发店洗,勤快的她于是代劳。

为女儿洗头,主要在女儿小的时候,女儿自己学会了洗头,朱艳群就放手了。

朱艳群为母亲洗头,已有数十年,至今还在继续,已然成了习惯。朱艳群说,老人为自己洗头,大约洗干净也不容易,去理发店吧,服务员可能也不会重视,还不如由她来为母亲洗,一则可洗得好一点,二则能给老人一点温情。

文章写到这里,我真有点惭愧,其实我是不该让朱艳群再为我洗头的,因为我有能力自己洗,也有条件上理发店洗。

朱艳群早早不为女儿洗头了,这是对的,可以早一点让女儿学会生活自理。朱艳群持续为母亲洗头,也是对的,老人是用来孝敬的。朱艳群再为我洗头却不妥,助长了我的懒惰,在这方面,我不该是她照顾的对象。从今往后,我不要她洗头了。让她自己给自己洗头吧,让她好好为母亲洗头吧。

# Hair-washing

Other than hair-washing laborers in the hair salon, Zhu Yanqun does more hair-washing than average people. She not only washes her own hair often, but also often washes my hair, her mother's hair and her daughter's hair when she was young.

That Zhu Yanqun does frequent hair-washing for herself can be attributed to three reasons. First, she is particular about personal hygiene. Second, she is practicing thrift by cutting down the expenditure on hair-washing in the hair salon. Third, she has invented a hairstyle that can be "done" exclusively by herself. The hairstyle has stayed unchanged for dozens of years and no hairdresser can do it.

Zhu Yanqun washes hair for me because I often neglect it, whether I wash it by myself or have it washed at the barber shop. She is so hard-working and helpful that she offers to do it for me.

As for washing the daughter's hair, it happened mainly when our daughter was young. Ever since our daughter learned to wash hair, Zhu Yanqun has stopped doing that.

It has been decades since Zhu Yanqun started washing hair for her mother, and it is still going on, having developed into a ritual. Zhu Yanqun has put it that if the old wash hair by themselves, it's no picnic to wash hair clean and if they go to the hair salon, the laborers are likely to take them lightly. So she had better do it for her mother. For one thing, she can wash hair cleaner; for the other, the elderly can feel some warmth from the young.

Writing this, I can't help feeling ashamed. In fact, I shouldn't have had Zhu Yanqun wash my hair, because I am able to do it by myself and I can afford to have it washed at the barber shop.

It's correct for Zhu Yanqun to stop washing her daughter's hair long ago in that it can foster her daughter's living independence earlier. It's also correct for Zhu Yanqun to keep washing her mother's hair because the elderly are to be respected and taken good care of. It is, however, not proper for her to wash my hair, because it has encouraged my laziness. On this aspect, I am no subject to her care. From now on, I will refuse her offer of washing hair for me. She might as well take her time to wash her own hair and her mother's hair.

## "上得厅堂"

"下得了厨房，上得了厅堂"，这是中国人赞美好女人的话。"人老珠黄不值钱"，这是中国老年人的感叹。在西方，七八十岁的老年人还在开车，开跑车的反而年轻人少，倒是老年人居多。中国人进入老年以后，别说开跑车了，就是"厅堂"也少上。这里的所谓"厅堂"，指的是社交场所，包括家里招待朋友的会客室。

人老了以后，如果只是在家里和老伴呆着，或接接孙子外孙，不和中青年交流，就会淡出主流社会，落伍于社会，不仅物理年龄和生理年龄老，而且心理年龄也会老。普通老百姓，七十岁已尽显老态；而那些高级领导、企业家、名人，七十岁却看上去精神得多。什么缘故？答曰：七十岁的老百姓只下厨房，不上厅堂；而七十岁的非普通老百姓，则少下厨房，多上厅堂。

为了让属于普通老百姓的母亲少下厨房，多上厅堂，朱艳群几乎禁止母亲干家务，家里来了客，通常邀请母亲到"厅堂"同坐，还不时启发母亲讲话，发表意见。有时外出交友，她也将母亲带去别家的厅堂。少下厨房，就可以少劳累，身体得到更好休息。多上厅堂，就可以活跃思维，享受精神愉悦，把老人的心理年龄降下来。朱艳群八十八岁的老妈，至今还能同年轻人愉快交流，实在是多上厅堂的功劳。

# "Up in the Hall"

"A good cook down in the kitchen, an elegant hostess up in the hall." It is a compliment for a good woman. "Old people are as worthless as yellow pearls." It is a common complaint by Chinese old people. In the West, the old in their seventies or even eighties are still driving. People who drive sports cars are mostly the old rather than the young. When the Chinese get old, they even don't enter the "halls", let alone the sports cars. Here the so-called "hall" refers to socializing places, including the living rooms where we receive guests.

When people grow old, if they just stay at home with their wives or go and pick up grandsons, without socializing with young people, they will fade from the mainstream society and fall behind the times. As a result, they tend to be older than their physical age, biological age and even psychological age. Ordinary people in their seventies always appear old with their bent back and unsteady steps, while those high-ranking officials, entrepreneurs and celebrities of the same age look much more energetic. Why? The reply is that seventy-year-old ordinary people don't go to the hall but the kitchen, but seventy-year-old non-ordinary people go to the hall more than to the kitchen.

To make her mother, one of the ordinary people, go to the hall more than to the kitchen, Zhu Yanqun almost forbids her mother from doing housework.

When the family has visitors, she normally invites her mother to the "hall" to join us. Besides, she also enlightens her mother from time to time so her mother can speak out and air her views. Sometimes when she goes out to socialize, she also takes her mother to her friends' living rooms. Going to the kitchen less, people can be less occupied with labor and be more physically relaxed. Going to the hall more, people can activate thinking and enjoy spiritual pleasure, as a result of which, the elderly people can be psychologically younger. It should definitely be owed to the practice of "going to the hall more" that Zhu Yanqun's eighty-eight-year-old mom can still have pleasant communication with young people today.

# 甜口良药

俗话说："良药苦口，忠言逆耳。"笔者曾经写过一篇题为《清富》的文章，说人们提倡的清贫只是比浊贫好，但不是最佳状态，最好是既清又富——清富。在此，我又想说，苦口良药只是比苦口毒药好，最好是甜口良药；逆耳忠言只是比逆耳奸言好，最好是顺耳忠言。

以为良药必定苦口，忠言必定逆耳，是一种思维定势，是片面的。就如"金玉其外"，不一定"败絮其中"一样，良药仅是往往苦口，忠言仅是往往逆耳。有了这样的觉悟，我们就会设法把良药做成甜品，把忠言说成顺耳的音乐。去年春天笔者突发心脏病，扬州的男性朋友发来顺耳忠言："保重龙体，我们还要'掼蛋'呢！""掼蛋"，一种扑克游戏矣。南通的女同事发来顺耳忠言："盼好好休养，早日归队。"前些天开车去杭州，在市中心不小心闯了红灯，见迎面而来的女交警，我停车"自首"，不料她说："以后注意就是了，我们警察有时疏忽偶尔也会闯红灯的。"这也是一句标标准准的顺耳忠言，听得我甚是感动，立志要把闯红灯的概率降到最低。

忠言可以说得顺耳，良药自然可以做得甜口。我家的朱艳群，就为其母亲常做一帖美味的良药。朱艳群的母亲多年来气血不足，引起心脏不适。中医为其配了三七、当归、人参磨成粉的保健药。朱艳群品尝过，觉得味不佳，便将此粉装入胶囊。这样苦味没了，但美味也无，每天吃也是一种负担。于是再改进，将此粉拌入咖啡加奶加糖，终于成了一道鲜美的甜品。看到早餐后的母亲品尝着自己独创的甜品，朱艳群笑得灿烂。

# Sweet Good Medicine

As a saying goes, "Good medicine is bitter, and faithful words grate upon the ear". I used to write an article entitled "White-handed Wealth", suggesting that white-handed poverty is only better than "filthy poverty" and is not the best condition. The best is being white-handed and wealthy, namely, white-handed wealth. Here, I would like to comment that bitter good medicine is only better than bitter poison. The best is sweet good medicine. Likewise, faithful words that grate upon the ear are only better than faithless words. The best are faithful words pleasing to the ear.

It's a stereotyped way of thinking to assume that good medicines are surely bitter and faithful words surely grate upon the ear. It's one-sided. Just as "fair skin" does not necessarily suggest "the multitude of sin", good medicines only tend to be bitter and faithful words only tend to grate upon the ear. With such awareness, we can manage to make good medicines into desserts, faithful words into pleasant music. Last spring, when I had a heart attack, my male friend in Yangzhou sent me a text message which was faithful words pleasing to the ear, "Take good care of yourself Your Majesty. We are going to play Guan Dan." Guan Dan is actually a card game. My female colleague in Nantong texted me other faithful messages pleasing to the ear, "Hope you have a good rest and return to our team soon." A couple of days ago, when I drove to Hangzhou, I ran the red light. Seeing the female traffic policewoman coming to me, I stopped my car to "confess my crime". To my surprise, she said, "So long as you don't do that again, it's no problem. As the police, we sometimes neglect the red light, too." Those were also genuinely faithful words pleasing to ears, by which I was greatly touched, and I was determined to minimize the chances of going against the red light.

Faithful words can be put in a pleasant way, so a good medicine also can be made sweet. Zhu Yanqun often makes for her mother a tasty good medicine. Her mother has suffered from insufficiency of vital energy and blood, which contributes to heart discomfort. Physicians of Chinese medicine prescribed for her health care medicine constituted by pseudo-ginseng, Angelica sinensis and ginseng which were ground into powder. After tasting it, Zhu Yanqun thought it didn't taste good, so she put the powder into capsules. In this way, there was no bitterness any more, but it was still not tasty and still posed a burden to eat every day. Then she made further improvement by mixing the powder into coffee and adding milk and sugar, and finally made it into a tasty dessert. Seeing her mother enjoy the dessert originated by her after breakfast, Zhu Yanqun was beaming with pleasure.

# 朱艳群读书

文如其人,衣如其人,读什么样的书亦如其人。

中国传统的读书人"尚文",以读人文书籍为主,少读科技书,少读工具书。西方人则"尚武",重科技,轻人文。中国人被"坚船利炮"打败以后,也走上了重科技、轻人文之路。如今的世界,人慢慢丧失自己原来的地位,变成机器的奴隶,变成电脑的附件。有识之士提醒我们,21世纪应该是教育学的世纪。这是个比喻,所谓教育学的世纪就是重新塑造人性的世纪,学校不仅培养生存技能,还要提高生命质量。这就要求多读哲学、文学、历史等人文书,少读科技书,少读工具书。据说,现在新华书店教辅材料、如何美容、怎样做菜之类的工具书销得好,文史哲的书籍销不动。这不是个好现象,与建设文化强国背道而驰。

近些年,抓家庭经济的朱艳群用于读书的时间和精力多些了。我发现,她倒是在补过去读"文史哲"少的课,除了重读《红楼梦》《水浒传》《三国演义》《西游记》,还读《战争与和平》《安娜·卡列尼娜》《傲慢与偏见》《红与黑》,还读唐宋元明清各朝代的演义,还读《老子》《论语》《墨子》等。

我很赞赏朱艳群读人文书籍,我还钦佩朱艳群读一种"工具书",那就是她母亲生什么病,她就研读有关治疗这种病的医学书。20多年前,她母亲患了心脏病，朱艳群就读《心脏病常识》，不仅了解此类病人该吃什么药，还掌握了平时饮食起居的适合方式。有种药叫"地奥"，朱艳群不知买了多少瓶给母亲吃，药效甚好。她母亲还患胆结石和骨质疏松，朱艳群也是有针对性地看书学习，了解治病知识，成了"半个医生"。

# Zhu Yanqun's Preference in Reading Books

The writing mirrors the writer, the clothing mirrors the wearer and the books one reads also mirrors the reader.

Traditional Chinese intellectuals "adore humanities". Their reading list was dominated by humanity books rather than science and technology and reference books. The westerners "adore science and technology", attaching great importance to science and technology rather than humanities. After the Chinese were defeated by western "ships and canons", China has adopted a route featured by "preference of science and technology to humanities". In today's world, people have gradually lost their original positions, reduced to slaves to machines and attachments to computers. Men of insights remind us that the 21st century is supposed to be one of education science. This is a metaphor. The so-called century of education science is a century that will re-mould humanity. Schools are expected to develop survival skills, and more importantly, elevate quality of life. This requires that people should read more philosophy, literature, history and other humanity books and fewer books of science and technology and reference books. It's said that now in Xinhua Bookstore, reference books on teaching and learning, how to improve looks and how to cook are selling well, while books on literature, history and philosophy encounter poor sales. This is not a good sign and goes against our aim of building China into a cultural power.

In recent years, Zhu Yanqun, our family finance manager, has spent more time and more energy reading. I notice that she is actually making up lessons that she has missed on reading "literature, history and philosophy". She has read *A Dream in Red Mansions*, *Heroes of the Marshes*, *Historical Romance of the Three Kingdoms* and *Journey to the West* again. Besides these, she also read *War and Peace*, *Anna Karenina*, *Pride and Prejudice* and *The Red and the Black*. In addition to historical romances of the dynasties including Tang, Song, Yuan, Ming and Qing, she also read *Laozi*, *The Analects of Confucius*, *Mozi*, etc.

I really appreciate the fact that Zhu Yanqun is reading books of humanities. I also appreciate her efforts to read another kind of "reference books". That is, once her mother suffers from any disease, she will study medical books on treatment of that disease. Twenty years ago, after her mother was diagnosed with heart disease, she started reading *Elementary Knowledge of Heart Disease*, from which she has got to know not only the specific medicine to be offered to patients with heart disease, but also the ways of living in the daily life appropriate to such patients. There is a medicine called "Di Ao". Zhu Yanqun has bought many bottles for her mother. The medicine turns out quite potent. And since her mother suffered from cholelithiasis and osteoporosis, Zhu Yanqun has been doing study reading to help cope with the diseases. She is so well acquainted with the knowledge concerned that she has become "half a doctor".

# 母亲的衣服

食、住、行,是动物的基本生存条件;衣、食、住、行,是人的基本生存条件。由此一比较,衣的重要性显而易见:它是区别于人与动物的一个标志。

解决温饱问题,温的问题主要体现在衣的上面。衣食住行,衣食排在住行前面,足见衣食在生存条件中的位置。衣又在食之先,说明人哪怕饿着肚子,也得穿上衣服。在公众场合穿上衣服,当是最起码的文明。

朱艳群虽然出身贫寒之家,但小时候衣服还是穿着整齐的。家里没钱去店里为小孩买新衣服,可她母亲学会了裁缝,又勤快,家中四个小孩一年四季的衣服全由母亲亲手缝制。朱艳群的母亲不仅衣服做得好,而且色彩搭配的审美眼光也好,做的衣服的颜色适合每个孩子的特点,比如两个儿子文静,衣服的色彩就比较素雅,两个女儿活泼,衣服的色彩就温暖、热烈。上下衣如何搭配,也特别讲究。并将这些简易、通俗的"色彩学"讲解给孩子们听。因此,朱艳群从小在自己的穿衣戴帽中学到了些许美学,为她日后学习印刷,装潢办公用房和家室,打下了艺术功底。

待到有能力抚养父母的时候,朱艳群全包了母亲的穿衣问题。当然,她没有如先前母亲为她亲制衣服一样为母亲做衣服,她只是去店里为母亲购买衣服。不过,她为母亲添衣,却是十分用心的。一是体现在数量上,每当季节转换,她总想到为母亲买新衣,每次出国或出远差,她也总不忘为母亲买衣服。二是体现在选择上,每次为母亲购衣,她总会认真挑选,从布料、色彩到款式,无不讲究,非挑到适合的不可。

　　朱艳群为母亲购的衣服,她母亲满意不满意呢?布料、色彩、款式每每满意,老太太常常不合意的是,嫌衣服太大,穿着影响了身材,说是"没了腰身"。朱艳群辩说,特意买大的,因你年龄大了,身材是否好看不重要,穿得宽松舒服才是硬道理。关于这一点,母女俩至今未达成一致。

# Clothes for Mum

Food, shelter and moving are basic living conditions of animals. Clothing, food, housing and transportation are basic living conditions of humans. As is shown through the comparison, the significance of clothing is evident: it's a distinction between humans and animals.

Speaking of getting full and warm, getting warm is mainly related to clothing. In the fixed term of "Clothing, food, housing and transportation", clothing and food rank before housing and transportation, which fully confirm the importance of clothing and food among the four living necessities. And clothing coming before food indicates that humans would rather stay hungry than stay naked. Being dressed in public is the minimum civilization.

Although Zhu Yanqun was born in a poor family, she was dressed neatly in her childhood. The family couldn't afford to buy from stores new clothes for the kids. But having learned to sew and being hardworking, her mother had made by hand for her four kids clothes to wear in four seasons of the year. Zhu Yanqun's mother not only sews well, but also has good aesthetic visions of color combination. Colors of the clothes for kids are right for each kid's characteristics. For example, for her two gentle and quiet sons, cool and quiet colors were used, and for her two lively and outgoing daughters, warm and vibrant colors were used. She also had deep insights into the matching of upper outer garments and down clothes. She even explained the simple and popular "color science" to her kids. So since her childhood, Zhu Yanqun has acquired some aesthetic knowledge from her own dressing, which laid artistic foundations for her future study in printing, and for furnishing the offices and houses.

When she was able to support her parents, Zhu Yanqun took on everything related to her mother's clothing. Of course, she didn't make clothes for mother as her mother did for her long before, but went to stores to buy clothes for her mother. However, she has taken great care in buying clothes for her mother. One is her concern about quantities of clothes. Every time the season changes, she always buys new clothes for her mother. And every time she goes abroad or to distant places on business, she always thinks of buying clothes for her mother. The other is her concern about the criteria in picking clothes. Every time she buys clothes for her mother, she will select carefully, being particular about fabrics, colors and styles and won't give up until find the ideal clothes.

Then is her mother satisfied with the clothes bought by Zhu Yanqun? She is always satisfied with the fabrics, colors and styles, but not the size. The elderly lady complains that the clothes are too large to flatter her figure, saying that "she has no waist with the clothes on". Zhu Yanqun argues that she did it on purpose, in that for the elderly, dressing loosely and comfortably is of much more significance than dressing slim. On this, the mother and the daughter have yet to reach an agreement.

# 鸟语花香

农村里花草树木多,鸟也多,环境美。城市里交通、商业发达,可常缺鸟语花香。如果在城市里有个鸟语花香的地方,就两全其美了。

朱艳群的舅舅在中央人民广播电台郑州广播大学当校长。小时候,朱艳群陪同母亲去过那所大学。学校地处郑州市区,校园内绿树成林,树多鸟多,身临其中,花香扑鼻而来,鸟鸣不绝于耳。朱艳群的母亲说,闹中取静,闹中有繁华,静中有鸟语花香,这才是生活的好所在。

小时候听了母亲的感叹,朱艳群日后选择住所有了方向。我家先是住在绿树成荫的运河边上,后又住在风景秀丽的五里湖畔,两个住所均在市郊,离繁华不远,又靠近自然,有花香又有鸟鸣。

朱艳群是个极致的人,为了讨母亲的好,她不满足于室外花草树木多多,还舍得花钱买了几十个带花的"盆景",把家里弄得像半个"植物园"。如何让母亲天天可以听到鸟鸣呢?朱艳群设计了一种开放的鸟笼,就是鸟笼里放着鸟喜吃的食物,但将鸟笼的门打开,以让更多的鸟飞来进食,因此也让母亲听到更多的鸟鸣。

# Singing Birds and Fragrant Flowers

In the countryside, as can be seen, plants such as flowers, grass and trees are flourishing, flocks of birds are flitting about in the sky and the surroundings are beautiful. In the city, developed as transport and commerce are, there is regrettable absence of singing birds and fragrant flowers. It would be like having the best of both worlds if there were places with singing birds and fragrant flowers in the city.

Zhu Yanqun's uncle used to serve as director of Zhengzhou Broadcasting College affiliating to Central People's Radio. When she was young, she used to accompany her mother there. The college was located in downtown Zhengzhou. On campus, green trees made groves, which attracted many birds. Exposed to the scene, people were greeted by strong fragrance of flowers and incessantly lingering sound of birds singing. Zhu Yanqun's mother said that it was an ideal dwelling place which kept quiet in a noisy neighborhood so people can experience the bustle and hustle of the noisy neighborhood and meanwhile enjoy the birds singing and flower fragrance in the quiet place.

Having heard her mother's comments in the childhood, Zhu Yanqun has had a very clear goal in her choice of dwelling places. My house was originally located on the side of the canal where green trees made pleasant shades. Then we moved to the lakeside of the picturesque Wuli Lake. Both houses are in the suburbs, not far from the bustling city and close nature, boasting both flower fragrance and birds singing.

Zhu Yanqun is a perfectionist. To meet her mother's preferences, she is not satisfied with the flourishing flowers, grass and trees outdoor, and has spent quite a fortune buying dozens of blossoming "potted plants", making our garden almost like a "botanical garden". Then how to make birds singing available to her mother every day? Zhu Yanqun designed a kind of open birdcage. She put in the cage what birds like to eat, and kept the door open so that more birds could fly in to eat. In this way, she has succeeded in making her mother enjoy more birds singing.

# 给玩具

我和朱艳群和而不同,在许多问题上我们有分歧、有矛盾、有争论。当然,我们更有英雄所见略同的地方。不给小时候的女儿买玩具,却常常给朱艳群的母亲买玩具,就是我们和而又同的一例。

在这个世界上,无论是中国还是外国,只要经济条件许可,大部分家长喜欢给自己未成年的孩子买玩具,比如男孩玩汽车模型之类,女孩玩洋娃娃之类。我曾和买玩具给小孩的家长交流过,问他们为什么要让小孩玩玩具,答案不外有二:一曰开发小孩动手能力,二曰让小孩玩得开心。我和朱艳群对这样的说法不以为然,在我们看来,小孩玩玩具,只会越玩越小,不利于其心智成熟。小孩子只有更多地围着成人转,更多地与成人交流,向成人学习,才会学到更多有用的东西,早日成人。

商店里出售的玩具,几乎一律摆放在"儿童区域",似乎玩具与成人无关,与老人绝缘。这是一个误区。在我和朱艳群看来,玩具是更适合成年人和老年人的。成年人学习和工作的压力大,玩玩具,可以放松心情,利于健康。老年人社会活动减少,比较寂寞和孤单,玩玩具可以活跃思维,防止老年痴呆,增进心情愉悦。女儿如今年近三十,年幼时围着父母转的她对玩具不感兴趣,父母是她最大的玩具。现在倒好,会买一个真人般大的娃娃放在家里玩。

从未给女儿买过玩具的朱艳群,却热心为母亲买玩具,从"塑料拼图"、"俄罗斯魔方"到"遥控汽车",不一而足,搬家时装了一大箱。去年母亲87岁生日,还带她去游乐场开"碰碰车",让老人尝尝开车的感觉,玩得老人笑口大开。

# Offering Toys

Zhu Yanqun and I are harmonious but different. On many issues, we have diagreements, conflicts and even arguments. Of course, we think alike on more issues. We didn't use to buy toys for our daughter in her childhood, but often buy toys for Zhu Yanqun's mother, which is one of the cases showing we are harmonious and think alike.

In this world, whether in China or in foreign countries, so long as they can afford, most parents like to buy toys for their kids, such as car models for boys and dolls for girls. I used to discuss with parents who bought toys for kids, asking them why they got kids to play with toys. They always replied that first, it can develop kids' abilities of working with hands; second, it can bring fun to kids. Zhu Yanqun and I don't think so. In our opinion, offering kids toys to play with will only make them more childlike, thus hindering their psychology and intelligence from further development. Only when kids stay more with adults, communicate more with adults and learn from adults can they learn more useful stuff and become mature in due time.

Toys for sale in stores are uniformly on display in "Children Areas", as if toys had nothing to do with adults and even totally irrelevant to the old. This is a misunderstanding. From our perspective, toys are more suitable for adults and the old. Adults are highly stressed from study and work, so playing with toys helps them relax and stay healthy. The old people have reduced social activities and tend to feel lonely, so playing with toys helps them activate thinking, avoid suffering from Alzheimers Disease and stay in a joyful mood. Our daughter is now nearly thirty years old. When she was young, she had no interest in toys and followed us a lot. Parents are her greatest toy. It is now, she, instead, would buy a life-sized doll to play with at home.

Zhu Yanqun, never having bought toys for her daughter, however, is keen on buying toys for her mother. Toys range from "Plastic Picture Mosaic" to "Tetris", "Remote Control Car", etc, to name just a few. When we moved to a new house, the toys had filled a large box full. On her mother's 87th birthday last year, she even took her to the amusement park and drove the bumper cars. It had given her a feeling of driving cars and made her burst into laughter.

# 泡电话

什么叫"泡电话",我的理解是:在电话里长时间说一些无关紧要的话。"泡电话"是时代的产物,取决于电话普及,话费便宜。

据观察,"泡电话"的主要有三类,一类是有闲的太太们,赚钱养家有丈夫顶着,她们闲来无事,便电话来电话去,在电话里闲聊,从美容、减肥、购物到自家先生到二奶,无话不聊,大谈特谈,谈聊无止。再一类是子女出国留学或在外地就读,做母亲的放心不下,牵肠挂肚,便在电话里问长问短,关照这关照那,唠叨个没完。第三类是谈情说爱的男女,他们在电话里互展其长,互诉衷肠,互表忠心,你表扬我,我夸奖你,或者你骗骗我,我诈诈你,好似智力竞赛。

朱艳群也"泡电话",不过她不在上述三类之中,第一,她不是"有闲阶级",第二,女儿就在身边。她"泡电话"属于另类,她只和自己的老妈"泡电话"。"父母在,不远行",朱艳群没能做到这一点,她每年都要出差、出国一些时间,不在母亲身边,无法和母亲一起散步、当面说话,她就借助电话,借助"泡电话",与母亲保持亲密接触,既关心母亲的身体、母亲的心境,又把外面世界的精彩和新鲜事告知母亲,与母亲分享。每天晚上长时间接听女儿来自远方的电话,成了朱艳群母亲的一大快乐。

# Hooked on the Phone

As to what is "being hooked on the phone", my definition is talking unimportant stuff on the phone for a long time. The phenomenon of "being hooked on the phone" is the product of this period and has resulted from the popularity of telephones and low telephone rates.

It's observed that people who are "hooked on the phone" fall into three groups. Group one are idle wives. Their husbands earn the bread and support the family, so being unoccupied, they have nothing to do but phone each other. They chat on the phone endlessly and excessively, with no topic taboos. Their topics range from improving looks, losing weight and shopping to husbands and their mistresses. Group two are mothers with children studying abroad or in other places. As mothers, they feel very worried and deeply concerned about their children, so they ask all sorts of questions on the phone, advising repeatedly and chattering endlessly. Group three are men and women who talk love. Talking on the phone, they display their strengths, confide in each other, commit mutual loyalty, compliment each other or hoax each other, which is like an intelligence contest.

Zhu Yanqun is also "hooked on the phone", but she belongs to neither of the first two groups. First, she is not an "idle wife". Second, her daughter is right by her side. Her "being hooked on the phone" is quite unique, for she is only "hooked on the phone" for her dear mother. As an old saying goes, "while the parents are alive, the children shouldn't travel to distant places." Zhu Yanqun can't fulfill this requirement, for she will be on business or be abroad for some time every year. Not by her mother's side and unable to walk and talk in person with her mother, she always uses the telephone and gets "hooked on the phone" to keep in close touch with her mother. In doing this, she can not only know her mother's health and emotion status, but also share with her mother the wonderful and interesting things taking place in the outside world. It has become her mother's great pleasure to receive Zhu Yanqun's long phone calls from a distant place every evening.

# 打麻将

有人说,麻将里面有辩证法。有人说,麻将如人生,手气好的时候是顺境,手气背的时候如逆境。有人说,打麻将,三分靠技术,七分靠手气;人的命运,三分靠运气,七分靠自己。因为打麻将太有意思吧,所以全国各地的人都喜欢。据说四川人最热爱这种游戏,成都上空的飞机尚未下降,就能听到地面上的麻将声。

我手很笨,7岁还不会穿衣服,为此常被幼儿园老师批评。可我也有聪明的地方,还是7岁那年,学会了收听"短波",常听当年禁听的"美国之音";学会了打麻将,常和成年人玩这种游戏。

从小学会了的东西,从小感兴趣的东西,长大以后一般不会放弃。工作再忙,我也会抽出时间和朋友们打麻将,当然属于"小来来",称不上赌博。记得女儿第一次对我提出批评,就是说我麻将打得太多。

朱艳群原先也是反对我打麻将的,理由是,常打麻将耗神耗体力,不利于健康;打麻将"小来来"也是有输赢,有输赢就是赌,是不良的娱乐活动。没想到,近些年,朱艳群也打起麻将来了,不过她只陪母亲玩,只陪母亲玩"零赌麻将",理由有两条:一是母亲有兴趣,二是听说打麻将可防老年痴呆,她陪母亲打麻将,相当于防病于未然。

# Playing Mah-jong

Some hold that there is dialectics involved in playing mah-jong. Some think that playing mah-jong is like living a life. When you get good cards, it's a favorable situation, and when you get bad cards, it's adversity. Others believe that winning a mah-jong game calls for thirty percent techniques and seventy percent luck; similarly, one's life is determined by thirty percent luck and seventy percent individual efforts. Maybe it's because playing mah-jong is very interesting that people across China all like it. The Sichuanese are said to be the keenest fans of this game. Before planes high above the Chengdu city begin to take off, it is said that people can even hear the sound of playing mah-jong on the ground.

I was so clumsy in using hands that I was unable to put on clothes until seven, for which I often got criticized by teachers at the kindergarten. But I also had something I was good at. Still at the age of seven, I learned to tune my radio to "short wave" programs and often received the then banned program of "Voice of America". Besides, I have learned to play mah-jong and often played it with adults.

When people grow up, they usually won't give up what they have learned and been interested in since their childhood. However busy I am at work, I always manage to find time to play mah-jong with my friends. Of course, it's only "small betting", and can't be called gambling. As I remember, the first time my daughter criticized me, she was complaining about me playing too much mah-jong.

Zhu Yanqun was originally against me playing mah-jong on the ground that it is energy-consuming and harmful to health. She also holds that even if it's "small betting", so long as it involves winning and losing, it's gambling, which is very unhealthy recreation. To my surprise, in recent years, Zhu Yanqun has also picked up this hobby. However, she only plays it with her mother, and only at "zero stake". The reasons are as follows: first, her mother is interested in it; second, it's said that playing mah-jong can help prevent Alzheimer's Disease. So it's like nipping the disease in the bud when she plays mah-jong with her mother.

# 父母的小店

上世纪80年代初,朱艳群的父母在老家无锡东湖塘镇上开了一家类似如今"可的"一样的小店,卖烟酒,卖小杂货。

今天回忆起来,朱艳群对父母的小店贡献不小。朱艳群对我说,关心和支持父母的小店,不仅是一个经济问题,也是一个对父母的孝敬问题,因为店开得好不好,不光跟收入有关,也跟父母的心情有关。

首先是帮助父母把店开起来。当年,社会上比较"左",个体户还不吃香。朱艳群和我给父母壮胆,告诉他们,发展个体经济大势所趋,是社会进步的需要,不光不丢脸,还是挺光荣的事。在父母打消了顾虑以后,朱艳群便积极"跑审批",终于在短时间内办妥手续,在镇上首开了个体小店。

其次是帮助进货。上世纪80年代是以计划经济为主,以市场经济为补充的年代,许多商品十分紧俏,进货成了难题。在此情况下,朱艳群几次三番"命令"我利用关系"走后门",采购"中华烟"等热销品。

再次是帮助销售。民营企业只求利润,不图GDP。朱艳群为了让父母开心,创作虚假的销售业绩。她请来几位朋友做"客户",买了很多烟酒,然后又以进货的名义,把销出去的烟酒倒回来。这种做法,颇有点国有企业"欺上"的味道。可用于家庭,似也无妨,而且有利而无弊。

# Parents' Store

In the early 1980s, Zhu Yanqun's parents owned a store in their hometown, Dong Hu Tang Town, Wuxi. The store is similar to today's chain grocery, "Ke Di", selling cigarettes, wine and groceries.

When we look back now, we find Zhu Yanqun had made quite a lot of contributions to the store. Zhu Yanqun told me that showing concern and support for parents' store was not only a matter of economy but also a matter of filial piety to parents, because besides income, what's also closely associated with the store's business was the parents' state of mind.

Her first contribution was helping her parents open the store. At that time, the society was very "left-leaning" and self-employed individuals were not popular. Zhu Yanqun and I encouraged her parents, convincing them that developing self-employed economy represented the general trend and needs of social progress. It was not disgraceful, but honorable. After her parents gave up the worries, Zhu Yanqun was actively engaged in "obtaining inspection and approval", and finally succeeded in completing all formalities within a short period of time and opening the first self-employed store in the town.

Her second contribution was helping purchasing goods for sale in the store. In the 80s which was featured by "planned economy dominating and market economy supplementing", many goods were in short supply and purchasing goods for sale was a hard nut to crack. Under these circumstances, Zhu Yanqun repeatedly "ordered" me to use my social connections to "get in by the back door" and to buy "Chung Hwa" and other salable goods.

Her third contribution was helping sell goods. Private businesses were but concerned about profits, not GDP. To delight her parents, Zhu Yanqun had created false sales achievements. She made her friends pretend to be "customers" and buy many cigarettes and wines. Then she bought back the cigarettes and wines in the name of purchasing goods for sale. In "deceiving the superiors", such a practice sort of resembled those state-owned enterprises. But adopted among families, the practice seemed to pose no harm and even brought many benefits.

# 接送车

在我们这个国家,在我们这个时代,官当到一定高度,离退休以后待遇不错,除了收入不低,还有许多"照顾",如外出有单位公车接送。前些天江苏人民广播电台已离休23年的老台长来无锡看望我,就是单位派专车送来的。

朱艳群的父母亲别说当官了,就连公务员也没当过,所以外出不可能有单位公车接送。好在他们生养了朱艳群这样的女儿,照样享受外出有车接送的待遇。

近30年来,朱艳群的父母一直跟随我们一起生活。朱艳群的两个哥哥和一个姐姐,分别住在三个不同的地方,有的在城市,有的在郊区,也有的在远乡。当父母的,总是把每个孩子放在心上,多会思念并希望常常见面相处,所以除了不居住在身边的子女来看望他们,他们过些时候也要去子女们那里走动走动。这个时候,朱艳群就派车让驾驶员又送又接。有时遇上公司用车紧张,几辆车排不过来,朱艳群宁愿自己坐出租车,也要确保父母的接送需求。

年老了,多怀旧,怀旧事,怀老友。朱艳群的母亲在娘家丹阳和上海等地都有年轻时很要好的朋友,平时写写信通通电话不过瘾,她就会提出要去看望,或者请他们前来做客,这就又用上了接送车。派车送派车接,朱艳群乐此不疲。她说,能为父母多做些什么,也是自己的一种幸福。

# Courtesy Cars

Nowadays, in our country, officials of quite high ranks enjoy good welfare and salaries after retirement. In addition to good salaries, there is much "preferential treatment". For instance, when they go out, the governmental institutions they previously worked for will send cars to serve as courtesy cars for them. A couple of days ago, the former director of Jiangsu People's Radio who has been retired for 23 years, visited me in Wuxi. He came in such a courtesy car.

Zhu Yanqun's parents have never been government employees, let alone government officials. So when they go out, there won't be any courtesy cars offered by the governmental institutions. Fortunately, they have such a capable daughter as Zhu Yanqun, so they also can enjoy the "special treatment" of a courtesy car offered by their daughter for commuting.

In the recent 30 years, Zhu Yanqun's parents have been living with us. Zhu Yanqun's two brothers and a sister live in three different places, one in the city, another in the suburbs and the other in distant villages. Parents are always concerned about every child, missing them and hoping to often see them in person. So after their children living elsewhere have come to visit them, they will pay a return visit. Then Zhu Yanqun will arrange for a driver to send and collect them. Sometimes when the cars are in short supplies, Zhu Yanqun would rather took a taxi herself and let her parents use the car.

The old people tend to be nostalgic, missing old things and old friends. In Dan Yang, her parents' home, Shanghai and other places, Zhu Yanqun's mother has got friends very close to her when they were young. Correspondence and phone calls can't satisfy their craving for meeting, so she will suggest going to visit her friends, or inviting them to visit her. Then here courtesy cars are in use again. Zhu Yanqun always enjoys arranging for cars to serve her mother. She says that it gives her happiness to do something for her parents.

# 发呆房

呆是笨和傻的意思，说别人呆子，有骂人的味道。可发发呆，又是挺惬意的，这里的呆，全无了笨和傻的含义。汉字啊，太美妙了。我是个国际主义者，对民族和国家看得没那么重，可我对中国的文字，情有独钟。我们中国当然有许多地方不如外国，但中国的文字绝对世界第一。那个英语，还世界语呢，我不仅不喜欢那26个字母拼成的东西，就连它的语法也有点反感。据出版社的编辑说，100页的中文加上英文翻译，变成了250页，可见，为了节省纸张，也是中文比英文好。

回到题目上来，说发呆房。多年前，朱艳群随一个新闻代表团访问台湾，其间应邀去一个友人家做客。留下深刻印象的，是主人家的发呆房。那个30平方米的发呆房面临大海，四壁白色，挂几幅书画，室内除了一把椅子和一个茶几，别无他物，坐在其中看看海，发发呆，真好！

朱艳群当时就想，要是让父母也有一个这样的发呆房，该多好啊。

2007年，我家装修新房，朱艳群果然请一名台湾设计师将二楼临水的一室做成发呆房，让有闲在家的父母，在此坐坐摇椅，喝喝咖啡，看看流水，发发呆。有一次，岳母对我说："天堂就在尘世，天堂就在家里的发呆房。"

# A Room for Sitting Idle

"Dai" in Chinese means "stupid" and "silly". Calling others "Daizi" has the implication of swearing. But "Fa Dai" (sitting idle) is quite leisurely and comfortable. "Dai" in "Fa Dai" is totally free of the implication of being stupid and silly. Chinese characters are really beautiful. I'm an internationalist, not regarding nations and countries as important, but I have special preference for Chinese characters. Indeed, China lags behind foreign countries in many aspects, but Chinese characters absolutely rank first in the world. As for the English language, although it's used worldwide, I don't like the stuff spelt with twenty-six letters, and even sort of averse to its grammar. According to one editor from a publishing house, a 100-page Chinese version, combined with English translation, has turned into a 250-page one. Obviously, in terms of saving paper, Chinese characters are better than English letters.

Let's get back to the title and discuss the room for sitting idle. Many years ago, Zhu Yanqun paid a visit to Taiwan as a member of a press delegation. During the time, she was invited to visit a friend's home. What impressed her a lot was a room for sitting idle. Overlooking the sea, that 30-square-meter room has four walls painted white, with some works of painting and calligraphy hung on the walls. There is nothing inside the room except for a chair and a tea table. How nice it would be to sit in the room, observing the sea and doing nothing!

An idea had then occurred to Zhu Yanqun that how nice it would be for her parents to own such a room for sitting idle.

In 2007 when we had our new house furnished and decorated, Zhu Yanqun did engage a designer from Taiwan to convert a room on the second floor which overlooks a stream into one for sitting idle. So when her parents are at leisure at home, they will sit in the rocking chairs, drinking coffee, observing the running water, and sitting idle. The other day, my mother-in-law told me, "Heaven lies in the earthly world; heaven lies in the idle room at home."

# 轮椅和轿子

轮椅和轿子颇有相似之处：轿子要人抬，轮椅通常要人推；轿子是代步工具，轮椅也是；坐在轿里被人抬，是被人伺候，坐在轮椅里被人推，是被人照顾。轮椅和轿子也大不同：坐轮椅的，一般身份不分贵贱；而坐轿子的，则分等级。就是婚嫁用的，也分层有档。

打倒了封建王朝，轿子也逐渐不见了，这很好。人人平等，不分贵贱，官员、富人坐在轿子里让人抬，实在不人道。那个"婚轿"也没意思，矫揉造作，新娘已是成年人，自己不会走吗？是不是也想过过做官做富人的瘾。

轮椅倒是好东西，它是老、弱、病、残者的福音，霍金离不开它，张海迪离不开它，今天和将来，许许多多的人离不开它。轮椅，是一部分人的生存工具，也是我们健康的人向身体的弱者献爱心的一样东西。

我们家也有一辆轮椅。女儿有一次伤了腿，偶尔用过几天，她妈朱艳群推过她，我也推过她。小时候抱她，她还不懂感激，如今推着坐在轮椅里的她，她一副很领情的样子。

我们家的轮椅是为朱艳群的母亲买的，当然是岳母坐的机会多，朱艳群、女儿、我推的时间多。我们陪老人散步，路短，就让老人自己行走，路远，就带上轮椅，让老人走走停停，再坐上轮椅，让我们推着她前行。这样很好，既让老人散步练了身体，又让老人坐在轮椅里享受"服务"，感受小辈的孝心。

# The Wheelchair and The Sedan-chair

There are quite a few resemblances between the wheelchair and the sedan-chair. The sedan-chair is lifted by others and the wheelchair is usually pushed by others; the sedan-chair is a means of transport, and so is the wheelchair; sitting in the sedan-chair lifted by others is a way of being waited upon, and sitting in the wheelchair pushed by others is a way of being taken care of. There are also differences in between. Wheelchair takers are normally not differentiated between statuses, but people sitting in sedan-chairs are. Even brides using the sedan-chairs are divided into high and low in terms of their ranks.

It's good to see after the overthrow of feudal dynasties, the sedan-chair gradually faded out of sight. People are equal, and not to be treated according to different ranks. It's really inhumane for the officials and the rich to sit in sedan-chairs lifted by others. As for the "wedding sedan-chair", it's also senseless and unnatural. As an adult, shouldn't the bride herself walk on her own feet? Is she satisfying her own craving for being an official or a rich person in this way?

But the wheelchair is good stuff. It's the happiness and benefit of the old, the weak, the sick and the disabled. Hawkin can't live without it, Zhang Haidi can't live without it, and many people can't live without it, now and in the future. The wheelchair is a tool for survival for some people, and a gift with which the healthy people show their love and care to the weak people.

There is a wheelchair now in our home. Our daughter had her leg injured and had used the wheelchair for a couple of days. Her mother had pushed her, and so had I. In her childhood, when we carried her in arm, she wasn't very grateful. But now when we pushed the wheelchair, she had a look of gratitude.

Our wheelchair was bought for Zhu Yanqun's mother. So mostly, she was sitting in it, and Zhu Yanqun, our daughter or I would push it. When we accompany her to walk, if it is near, we would let her walk, and if it is far, we would take our wheelchair so she could sit in the wheelchair after a long walk and we would push her forward. This practice can both enable the old people to keep fit by walking and make them enjoy "service" in the wheelchair and feel filial piety from the young generations.

## 看话剧

在所有的剧种当中,我只喜欢话剧。与其他剧种相比,话剧最接近于电影,喜欢看电影的必然喜欢话剧。较之其他剧种,话剧又最接近于生活,热爱生活的人应当热爱话剧。

喜欢看电影,又喜欢反映真实生活的文学作品的我,自然喜欢上了话剧。和电影演员相比,话剧演员更不简单,他们直接面对观众,是"直播",不容犯错。电影则是"录播",错了可以改,不理想可以重来。所以,话剧演员更要有扎实的功底。

话剧里说的话一般是普通话,应该是所有观众能够听懂的,而且演员技能又不差,加上演员与观众面对面,加上反映现实生活,有此几条,想来话剧是百姓喜闻乐见的。可实际情形并非如此,在当今中国社会,话剧没什么市场,除了北京、上海、天津等几个大城市话剧观众能养活话剧场和话剧演员,在其他城市,话剧观众寥寥。前些年南京市曾有过话剧演出,可存活期短短。其他中小城市和农村,更没有话剧的容身之地。

话剧没有市场,我不信是因为没有好作品和好演员,原因只有一条,就是好的观众太少。周立波说,现在读书的人比写书的人还少。读书的人少,必然是喜欢看话剧的人少,话剧不仅跟电影接近,还跟书籍接近。一个社会人文状况怎么样,只需看两条:一条是读书的人多不多,一条是看话剧的人多不多。

许多人相信,上一代人和下一代人有代沟,我不反对这样的说法,但在我看来,人与人之间的"人沟",更突出,更要紧,更本质。代沟,随着时间的推移,容易填平;"人沟"问题,即文化差异,价值观差异,实难解决。

朱艳群的母亲、朱艳群和我及女儿,是三代人,就因为我们"人沟"浅,所以少有代沟。我们三代人都喜欢看话剧,就是一个例证。话剧演出离无锡最近的,是在上海。我们三代人常去上海,不为别的,就为去观看话剧。《一对小夫妻》《争吵与和平》《白领房奴》等一批话剧节目,我们都没有错过。朱艳群的母亲说,看话剧,既能饱眼福,又能如读书,"开卷"有益。

# Watching the Stage Play

Among all genres of plays, I like the stage play only. Compared with other genres, the stage play is the closest to the movie, and a movie-lover will surely love watching the stage play. Compared with other genres, the stage play is also the closest to life, so a life-lover shall love the stage play.

I like watching movies and reading works of literature reflecting the real life, so I have automatically developed love for the stage play. Compared with movie actors, stage actors are quite something. They have face-to-face communication with the audience. It's "live" broadcast and allows for no mistake. Anyway, movies are "recorded" broadcast. Corrections can be made if any mistake occurs and the whole thing can be done again if the results are not good. So, it's more urgent for stage actors to have a solid foundation in acting.

The utterances in the stage play are usually mandarin which all the audience can understand. Besides, the actors' acting is quite strong, the actors and the audience are face to face, and the play is reflection of the real life. Given these factors, the stage play is supposed to be loved by the masses. But that's not the case. In today's China, the stage play hardly has any market. Except in Beijing, Shanghai, Tianjin and other big cities where the audience can support the theatre and actors, audiences in other cities are scanty few. Years before, there had been stage plays put on in Nanjing, but the survival time was really short. As in other medium-sized and small cities and in the countryside, there is even no market at all for the stage play.

That the stage play has no market, I don't think, should be owed to the lack of good works and good actors. There is only one reason, that is, lack of good audiences. Zhou Libo the comedian has put it that nowadays readers are even outnumbered by writers. Just as there are few readers, there will surely be few fans of the stage play. The stage play is not only close to the movie, but also close to the book. The current humanity condition of a society is usually subject to two criteria: one is the number of people who read, and the other is the number of people who watch the stage play.

It's universally believed that generation gap does exist between two generations. I'm not against this belief. But in my opinion, "individual gap" between individuals is more distinct, more urgent and more essential. As time goes by, the "generation gap" can be bridged easily. However, the "individual gap", namely, differences in culture and values, is hard to be bridged.

Zhu Yanqun's mother, our daughter, Zhu Yanqun and I are three generations. The "individual gap" among us is not deep, so the "generation gap" hardly exists. It is a case in point that we all like watching the stage play. The nearest venue of the stage play to Wuxi city is in Shanghai. We often go to Shanghai for the sole purpose of watching a stage play. And we have watched "A Young Couple", "Quarrel and Peace", "White-collar House Slaves" and other plays. Zhu Yanqun's mother said that watching stage plays can both bring visual enjoyment and, as reading does, nourish the mind.

# 一种游戏

人生来之不易，游戏人生是不行的，可人生倘若缺少了游戏，则乏味得多，所以游戏还是要的，还是有正面意义的。别说人了，就是动物，在解决了温饱之后，它们也会用各自的方式游戏一番。我们常见的狗和猫，它们就会自己跟自己玩或跟同类玩。猫还能跟自己的猎物——老鼠玩，捉捉放放，放放又捉捉。乌鸦智商颇高，游戏的花样就更多，如空中翻跟斗，如单脚挂在树枝上荡秋千，如在空中把衔着的小树枝吐出，然后俯冲下来再咬住。

人的游戏自然更多，更高级，既有娱乐性，又有智力性。不同年龄、不同文化层次、不同兴趣的人，各有各的游戏方式。记得小时候，男孩普遍玩玻璃球，女孩普遍玩跳橡皮筋。如今，玩高尔夫，玩卡拉OK，成了一些人的时尚。

高龄的母亲玩什么游戏好呢？朱艳群将此作为一个课题来思考。有一次，我在台上玩一种"弹棋子"的游戏，就是在台子的一端放一枚棋子，再用另一粒棋子将它撞出台面。两粒棋子均出台面，为"和"；把对方的棋打下去，自己的棋留在台面上，为赢；对方的棋还在台上，自己的棋却下台了，为输。这种游戏体力消耗少，所弹之手一弹一收之间又能活络手指，舒筋活血。朱艳群觉得这种游戏非常适合老年人，便推荐给母亲。她母亲果然喜欢上了这种游戏，平时一个人常常自己练练、玩玩，居然"棋艺"大增，朱艳群、我及女儿都不是她的对手，几乎每次都输给她。

# A Game

Life is precious. It's not good to treat life as a game. But without games, our life then becomes less interesting and fun. Even animals would play games in their own ways after being warm and full, let alone humans. Such popular animals as dogs and cats would play with themselves or with other similar animals. Cats can even play with mice, their prey, a kind of catching and releasing game. The crow is rather intelligent, and can play a variety of games, such as doing a somersault in the sky, hanging off a branch and swinging, or spitting out the twig in the mouth in the sky and then diving down and gripping the twig with teeth again.

Surely humans can play more games, which are more advanced, more entertaining and more demanding on intelligence. People of different ages, education backgrounds and interests play different games. As I remember, in my childhood, boys all played with glass marbles, and girls all played skipping over rubber bands. Now, playing golf and Karaoke are fashion for some people.

What game suits the elderly mother then? Zhu Yanqun took it seriously as a project. The other day, I was playing a game called "flicking the chessman" on the chess table. The rule is that the player puts one chessman on one end of the table, and then flicks it out of the table with another chessman. If both chessmen get out of the table, it's a "tie"; if the opponent's chessman gets out while the player's own remains on the table, the player is winning; if the opponent's chessman remains on the table while the player's own gets out, the player is losing. Little energy consumption is involved in this game. What's more, fingers get exercised, muscles get relaxed and blood circulation gets stimulated while the hand is performing the action of flicking and drawing back. Zhu Yanqun found the game ideal for the elderly, and recommended it to her mother. Her mother just fell in love with the game as expected. In her spare time, she usually enjoys herself with this game. Practice makes perfect, and she ends up being very good at it. Her "chess skills" are so superb that Zhu Yanqun, my daughter and I are all defeated by her every time we play the game with her.

## "老人房"

房子问题历来是民生的大问题。

在我们中国,计划经济年代,城市人的住房是单位分配的,地位高的人分得大一点,楼层好一点,地位低的人分得小一点,楼层差一点。所谓大一点,就是大套,三房一厅。所谓小一点,就是竖套或单间,竖套是一大一小两个房间,单间就是一个房间。在大套和竖套之间,还有一种叫横套,就是有两个大房间。地位不高不低的,一般是单位里的中层,就分得这样的套型。所谓楼层好一点,就是三楼和四楼。当年的公配住房通常建六层,没有电梯,故五层、六层太高,尤其是六层,既高,又顶天,冬冷夏热,一层、二层太低,尤其是一层,既低,又立地,潮湿又不安全。

上世纪90年代市场经济以后,取消了住房分配,住房商品化,住大住小,住好住差,一律以钱说话,比如地段好的房子贵,面积大的房子贵,有了电梯,即楼层越高越贵。

朱艳群的父母不算太老、生活可以自理的时候,我们替他们买了一套商品房。进入80岁以后,我们便把一对老人接来同住,三代同堂。对高龄的老人,楼层不是越高越好,而是越低越好,底层最好。新世纪以来,商品房的质量大大提高,底层不再潮湿。我家的新房有一层和二层,原先卧室全在楼上,楼下仅有客厅、餐厅和厨房。为了适合老人居住,我们在一楼进行改造,在朝南有窗的位置做了一个"老人房"。朱艳群的父母住在"老人房",不用走楼梯。楼上住着女儿、女婿和外孙女,日常生活和老人有分有合,既有各自的空间,又便于照应。住在这样的"老人房"里,朱艳群的父母感觉方便、舒适,心里踏实。

# Rooms for the Old

Housing has always been a big problem related to the people's livelihood.

In China, back in the era of the planned economy, townsmen had flats allotted by the government institutions or state-owned enterprises they worked for. Employees of higher official ranks got larger flats which were on better floors, while employees of lower or no official ranks got smaller ones which were on worse floors. The so-called larger flats were large-sized, with three bedrooms and one living room. The so-called smaller flats fell into double-room flats and single-bedroom flats, the former having one large bedroom and one small bedroom, and the latter with a single bedroom. In terms of built-up area, there was another house type between the choices of large-sized flats and double-room flats, with two large bedrooms, called horizontal-shaped flats. Employees with middle-level ranks were normally allotted such a house type. And the so-called better floors refer to the third and fourth floor. In those days, the buildings allotted by the government were normally six floors tall with no elevators. So the fifth and sixth floors were too high. Especially the sixth floor, besides being the highest, it's the top floor, thus being cold in winter and hot in summer. And the ground and first floors were too low. Especially the ground floor, besides being the lowest, it's the bottom floor, thus being too damp and unsafe.

Since the implementation of market economy in the 90s, flat allotment has been cancelled. Houses are commercialized, so when people buy houses, money uniformly has the final say in the size and quality of houses. For example, houses with good locations are expensive, large houses are expensive, and after elevators are in use, the higher floor houses are located on, and they are more expensive.

When Zhu Yanqun's parents were still young enough to take care of themselves, we bought for them a flat at the market price. After they were eighty, we took them to our house to live with us. So the three generations lived under one roof. For the very elderly people, in terms of which floor to live on, it's not the higher the better, but the opposite, and the ground floor is ideal. Since the beginning of the new century, quality of houses built and sold by real estate developers has improved greatly. The ground floor is not damp any more. Our new house has the ground floor and the first floor. Originally, bedrooms were all upstairs, and there are only a living room, a dining room and a kitchen. To cater to the old people's needs, we had part of the ground floor remodeled, building a "room specially for the old" against the south-facing wall with a window on it. Thus Zhu Yanqun's parents are able to live in the room without using the stairs. Their daughter, son in law and granddaughter live upstairs. There is separation and union in our daily life. On the one hand, we have our respective space; on the other, it's convenient for us to look after them. Living in such a "room for the old", Zhu Yanqun's parents feel convenient, comfortable and secure.

# 三陪母亲

不知哪年哪月起,中国出现了一个叫做"三陪小姐"的群体,"三陪小姐"有兼职的,也有专职的。兼职的"三陪小姐"白天在单位上班,下班后和节假日去娱乐场所和专职的"三陪小姐"一样,陪男性客人喝酒、唱歌,再"出台"陪睡。由于金钱的诱惑,多有兼职转专职,少有专职转兼职。"三陪小姐"在社会上批评者众,同情、认可者寡,还时不时受到有关部门打击。说她们"三陪"之为无罪的,发声最大的是我们的全国人大代表、著名性学研究者、可爱的李银河女士。

"文革"期间另有"三陪"现象,那就是斗"走资派",有陪斗;让"反革命"游街,有陪游;枪毙"牛鬼蛇神",有陪枪毙。

如今的官场上也有"三陪",上级领导来了,下级不仅要迎来送往,还要陪吃、陪会、陪玩。迎来,要到出发地去接;送往,要送到下一站。吃,要吃山珍海味;会,尽说些空话、大话、假话和"正确的废话";玩,俗的多,雅的少,离文化甚远。

"三陪小姐",是一个有争议的问题;"文革"中的"三陪",荒唐之极;"三陪"领导,是腐败之风。

这里说说朱艳群三陪母亲。朱艳群的母亲体弱多病,去医院就医是常有的事,不管大病小病,朱艳群总要陪同前往医院查病、治病。有时需要住院，朱艳群还"陪床"。此为一陪。朱艳群的母亲有两个老家，一在镇江丹阳，一在无锡锡山区，每每母亲回老家，朱艳群也乐意"陪回"。此为二陪。人老了，用餐就慢，朱艳群的母亲也不例外。据观察，朱艳群平时一次用餐时间大约是15分钟。可只要和母亲一起用餐，她的用餐时间便成了半个多小时，因为母亲要半个多小时才能吃完，她是在饭桌上陪吃。此为三陪。

　　社会上的种种"三陪"名声不怎么好。朱艳群三陪母亲，倒是值得称道，应当仿效。

# Escort to Mum in Three Ways

There is no record as to when the group of "Escort Girls" (girls providing escort services including eating, singing and dancing, or by tacit agreement, providing sexual services) came into being in China. There are both part-time and full-time "Escort Girls". Part-time "Escort Girls" have fixed jobs in the daytime. After work and on holidays, they go to entertainment clubs, accompanying male guests drinking, singing and then sleeping, namely, "calling on sexual service", like those full-time girls. Due to the temptation of money, there are numerous cases of part-time girls changing to be full-time, but rare cases of the other way round. In the society, critics of "Escort Girls" greatly outnumber sympathizers. And "Escort Girls" are subjects to crack-down of the authorities concerned from time to time. The firmest defender of this group, claiming "Escort Girls" are innocent in offering the "three escort services", is the lovely Ms. Li Yinhe, Deputy to the National People's Congress and a famous scholar on sexology.

Another "three escort services" phenomenon occurred during the "Cultural Revolution". That is, escort to "capitalist-roader" when they were denounced at a public meeting, escort to "counter-revolutionaries" when they were paraded through streets, and escort to "class enemies" when they were executed.

Currently in the official circles, there are "Escort Officials" as well. When the officials of a higher rank pay an inspection visit, in addition to welcoming them and seeing them off, the subordinates also need to serve as escort to banquets, meeting rooms and entertainment places. Welcoming them involves picking them up from the places of departure, and seeing them off requires sending them to their next visiting place. Banquets always can't be without table delicacies from land and sea; meetings always can't be free from empty talk, big talk, false talk and "correct nonsense"; as for entertainments, vulgar entertainments greatly outnumber refined ones, rather far from being cultured.

The issue of "Escort Girls" is controversial, the issue of "Escort in the cultural revolution" is highly ridiculous, and the issue of "Escort Officials" is simply a corrupt practice.

Here are stories about how Zhu Yanqun serves as escort to her mother in three ways. Zhu Yanqun's mother is in ill health and thus a regular visitor of hospitals. Whether the illness is serious or minor, Zhu Yanqun always manages to accompany her to hospital for examination and treatment. When there is need to be in hospital, Zhu Yanqun will "accompany her at the bedside". This is her escort to mother in the first way. Zhu Yanqun's mother has two native places, one in Dan Yang, Zhen Jiang, the other in Xi Shan District, Wu Xi. Every time her mother goes there, Zhu Yanqun is willing to "accompany her back home". So this is escort to her mother in the second way. The old tend to dine rather slowly. Zhu Yanqun's mother is no exception. It's observed that it normally takes Zhu Yanqun around fifteen minutes to have a meal. But provided she has a meal with her mother, the time she spends in dining usually extends to half an hour or more, because it takes her mother more than half an hour to finish a meal, and she is accompanying her on the table. This is escort to her mother in the third way.

The various "Escort" services in the society have rather bad reputations. But Zhu Yanqun's escort to her mother in three ways deserves praise and we should follow her example.

# 下午茶

身在欧洲的英国,好像有意要和其他欧洲国家有所区别,保持距离。去欧洲旅游,办个申根签证,可以跑好多国家,英国却去不了,去英国得单独签证。欧元也是这样,好多欧洲国家参与了,英国却要例外。欧洲人大多以喝咖啡为主,英国人偏和亚洲人一样,以喝茶为主,尤其爱喝下午茶。"英国下午茶",成了一个专有名词。

中国人的传统是喝茶的。不过随着对外开放,喝咖啡的人日益多起来了,而且成了一种时尚。上岛咖啡、迪欧咖啡、两岸咖啡、啡度咖啡、咖啡国度等品牌咖啡店如雨后春笋在中国的大小城市开办起来。不过中国人毕竟是中国人,泡咖啡店的人,喝茶的还是大大超过喝咖啡的,中国人去咖啡店,大多是喜爱那西式的餐饮环境。

在中国,一个城市咖啡店多不多,往往是这个城市发达不发达的一个标志。咖啡店通常不是解决"饱"的地方,而是精神享受的地方。人们只有温饱了以后,才有闲情逸致去咖啡店喝咖啡或喝茶,在那里读读书,发发呆,会会朋友聊聊天。

传统意义上的咖啡店和茶室,在广东比较少见,广东多的是茶餐厅,即有茶喝,但更主要的是"餐",是吃饱肚子的地方,广东人似乎从来都不需要光喝咖啡或光喝茶的场所。广东人的这个特性,可能全世界少有。

中国人比外国人重视吃,广东人尤甚,广东人什么都敢吃,吃的品种人类第一,比如猴脑,比如乳猪。喜欢吃的广东人,为什么独独不喜欢单单喝咖啡或喝茶,我弄不明白。

话扯远了,本文的主题是要说朱艳群安排年老的母亲喝下午茶。无锡有两家咖啡店很是不错,一家在阳光花园,名叫咖啡国度,一家在奥林花园,名为啡度咖啡。这两家店不仅硬件一流,装潢美丽,而且服务水准高,身临其中,享受是美妙的。去过这两家店的朱艳群,灵机一动,想到让母亲每天下午来此喝喝下午茶或咖啡,是适合的。她母亲过去以后,果然喜欢。从此,老人常常中饭后先午睡片刻,接着就去泡咖啡店,在那里边喝边看报纸、读杂志,或看看窗外的风景,或和年轻的服务员说说话。我问岳母,在咖啡店感觉如何? 她说,咖啡店什么都好,她喜欢,只有一点遗憾,那就是咖啡店里少有和她一样的老人。

咖啡店里少有老人,这是我们中国的一个社会问题。

# Afternoon Tea

Although located in Europe, UK seems to try to distinguish itself from other European countries and keep distance on purpose. If you go traveling in Europe, after you apply for a Schengen visa, it can be used in many countries, but not in UK which requires another visa. The same is true with Euro. Many European countries have joined the Eurozone, but UK is an exception. Most Europeans have coffee as the main drink, but the English, like the Asians, just mainly drink tea, particularly the afternoon tea. "English Afternoon Tea", thus, becomes a proper name.

It's the Chinese tradition to drink tea. But with the reform and opening of our country, the number of people drinking coffee is growing. Drinking coffee has become a fashion. UBC Coffee, Dio Coffee, Cross Strait Café, Feeldom Coffee, Coffee Nation and other cafés have sprung up like mushrooms in large and small cities in China. However, after all, Chinese are Chinese. In the Café, people who drink tea still outnumber people who drink coffee. Most Chinese visit cafés because they like the western-styled dining atmosphere.

In China, the number of cafés in a city could be a criterion in judging whether a city is advanced or not. Cafés normally are not places where people get rid of "hunger" but where to have spiritual enjoyment. Only after people have enough to eat and wear are they in leisurely and carefree mind to visit cafés, drinking coffee or tea, doing some reading, sitting idle or chatting with friends.

Cafés and tearooms in the traditional sense are rare in Guang Dong Province. There are more tea restaurants here, namely, serving tea, and mainly "dinner". They are places for people to get full. The Cantonese seem never to need places solely serving coffee or tea. Worldwide the very characteristic of the Cantonese might be unique to them. The Chinese take eating more seriously than foreigners do, the Cantonese in particular. They dare to eat anything, and in terms of eating varieties, such as monkey brain and suckling pigs, may surpass all other regional groups of the human kind. Why do the Cantonese, who are so fond of eating, just not drink coffee or tea only? That's something I remain puzzled about.

We've gone too far from the topic. The theme of this article is about how Zhu Yanqun arranged for her elderly mother to enjoy afternoon tea. There are two cafés that enjoy quite good reputations, one in Sunshine Garden, named Coffee Nation, and the other in Aolin Garden, named Feeldom Coffee. Both boast first-class facilities and beautiful decoration, and offer high quality service. Being there, visitors can enjoy themselves very well. Zhu Yanqun has been to both cafés and got a sudden idea that it is good to invite her mother to drink afternoon tea or coffee every afternoon. After one visit, her mother liked the places as expected. Since then, she often takes a nap after lunch, and then goes to spend the whole afternoon in the cafés, reading newspapers and magazines, observing the views outside the window or chatting with the young waiters over a cup of tea or coffee. I asked her how it felt in the café. She said she liked cafés. Everything is perfect except for one thing she feels regretful about, that is, there rarely are elderly visitors like her in the cafés.

It is actually a social problem in China that we can rarely find elderly customers in cafés.

# 养鸡

我们家不养猫不养狗,却养鸡。我还写过一篇批评养狗的文章,题目叫《养狗的不是》,例举宠物狗的四条罪状:一曰咬人,二曰不卫生,三曰与人争粮食,四曰破坏人际关系。前三条不言自明,这第四条也许有人不理解,需道白:狗这种东西,不明是非,只要是主人,它就忠,就听话。长期养狗的人发现,狗的这种"优点"人不具备,于是对狗的感情日增,对人的情感慢慢淡化,平时宁愿喂狗、遛狗,也不愿和人喝茶聊天。长此以往,人变得冷漠、孤僻、忧郁、不近人情。

养鸡的好处,在我们家不光是养殖意义上的,即有产出,还有把鸡当朱艳群母亲宠物的价值。早晨起来把鸡从鸡窝里放出来,一天几次给鸡喂食,傍晚时分将鸡引回窝,是老人的必修课。观察鸡的日常生活和习性,是老人的乐趣。收获母鸡下的蛋,是老人的成就。

我们家共养了六只鸡,两公四母。鸡和狗一样,通人性。它们见到生人会躲,见到不喂它们食的主人无动于衷,不躲也不跟,见到天天喂它们食的朱艳群的母亲则紧跟不舍,一副亲热状,自然其中也有讨食的功利成分。岳母不止一次对我说,鸡是很聪明的,比如知道天黑了要回家,比如认识回家的路,比如会把前来争食的麻雀赶走,比如生了蛋会报功,比如懂得谁人对它好,比如在食的问题上公鸡会"女士优先",比如遇上危险,公鸡会保护"女性",比如公鸡之间会争风吃醋抢"女人",等等。岳母对我说,人的最高学问是哲学,身为动物的鸡也有哲学,你如有兴趣仔细研究,可以写一本题为《鸡的哲学》的书,这本书一定大有意思。由此看来,朱艳群的母亲养鸡养出情趣来了。我们让她养鸡,倒成了一种孝敬。

# Keeping Chicken

In our home, we don't keep cats or dogs, but chickens. I used to write an article entitled "The Demerits of Keeping Dogs", criticizing dog-keeping and listing four charges of pet dogs, namely, biting people, being unhygienic, competing with people for food, and damage interpersonal relationship. The first three charges are self-evident. As for the fourth, some people may not understand. It needs to be pointed out bluntly that dog can't distinguish right from wrong and is always loyal and submissive to its owner. People who keep dogs over a long time find that humans don't have this "merit" exclusive to dogs, so their affection for dogs grows day by day, while emotion for humans weakens gradually. Ordinarily, they would rather feed and walk dogs than drink tea and chat with humans. If things go on like this, people may become unconcerned, unsociable, depressed and unreasonable.

In our home, the values of keeping chickens are more as pets for Zhu Yanqun's mother than as food for the whole family. It's the elderly lady's obligatory course to set free chickens out of the chicken coop in the morning, feed chickens several times during the day and lead the chickens back into the coop at dusk. It's the elderly lady's pleasure to observe chickens' life habits. And it's the elderly lady's achievement to harvest eggs laid by hens.

We have kept six chickens, including two male and four female. Like dogs, chickens can read human facial expressions and gestures. They stay away from strangers and are indifferent to owners who don't feed them, neither avoiding nor following the owners. But they affectionately follow Zhu Yanqun's mother, the regular feeder everywhere. Of course, there is practical intention of begging for food involved in the following up. My mother-in-law has repeatedly told me that chickens are smart. For example, they know it's time to go home when it's getting dark. They know the way home. They will drive away the sparrows scrambling for food. They will report achievement when they lay eggs. They know who is good to them. And on food issues, cocks will adopt the "lady first" principle. In danger, cocks will protect "females", and may fight for "women's favor", etc. My mother-in-law told me that human's highest knowledge is psychology, and chickens, animals as they are, also have psychology. If I am interested in closer research, I can write a book entitled "Psychology of Chickens". The book must be of much fun. It seems that Zhu Yanqun's mother has cultivated her own interest and taste in chicken-keeping. Thus it has become a token of our filial piety to let her keep chicken.

# 种菜如养花

上世纪50年代，在北京十三陵水库劳动时，毛泽东、刘少奇、周恩来、朱德等中央领导曾分别题词，这些题词其他都忘了，唯朱德的题词至今还记得："劳动万岁。"劳动万岁，说得好！人是不会万岁的，圣人也好，伟大领袖也好，百岁就算长命了，呼他们万岁，或是个人崇拜，或是被统治者逼着说的违心话。劳动倒千真万确该万岁的。一则劳动是创造财富的必须，没有劳动，人会饿死、冻死。二则，劳动是快乐和幸福的源泉，是精神生活的必须。人只有通过劳动，包括体力和脑力的，才能实现自身的价值。假如物质丰厚，但无所事事，无所作为，那必定快乐不起来，充其量只能当一只快乐的猪，决计不会有这种快乐的人。

基于上述对劳动的认知，朱艳群让年老的父母也做一些力所能及且有情趣的劳动。种菜，就是朱艳群向父母建议的一种劳动。我家住郊区，家里有个小院子，适合在种树种花种草的同时种一点菜。

朱艳群的父母过去没有务过农，种菜是外行。朱艳群特意请来附近菜农手把手指导，教会父母种几样绿叶蔬菜，像青菜、大蒜、丝瓜什么的。当我们全家亲口吃到父母亲手栽种的菜，夸奖新鲜好吃又有机，老人着实开心。朱艳群的母亲说，种菜如养花，菜和花一样有观赏价值。种菜又胜养花，菜还有食用价值。种菜这样的劳动真好，应该万岁！

# Raising Vegetables as Flowers

In the 1950s, while working in Beijing Ming Tombs Reservior, Mao Zedong, Liu Shaoqi, Zhou Enlai, Zhu De and other leaders from the central government had written inscriptions. I have forgotten all other inscriptions except for one by Zhu De which says "Long live labor". Well put! A human being won't be ten thousand years old. Be it a saint or a great leader, being as old as one hundred can simply be counted as long-lived. As for paying to them tributes of "be ten thousand years old", it is either out of personality cult or because people are forced to utter these words against conscience. It's labor that actually should live long. First, labor is the requisite of wealth creation. Without labor, people may be starved or frozen to death. Second, labor is the source of enjoyment and happiness, a necessity of spiritual life. Only through labor, both physically and mentally, can people realize their self-value. Given the abundance of material resources, but with doing and achieving nothing, people won't be happy. He or she would at best count as a happy pig rather than a happy human being.

In view of the above interpretation of labor, Zhu Yanqun gets the elderly parents to do some interesting manual work within their power. Planting vegetables is one of the work Zhu Yanqun has suggested to her parents. We live in the suburbs. We own a small garden ideal for planting vegetables in addition to trees, flowers and grass.

Zhu Yanqun's parents haven't done any farming before and are really amateurs in planting vegetables. Zhu Yanqun has deliberately invited the nearby vegetable growers to offer specific tutoring and her parents have learned to plant quite a few green leafy vegetables, such as Bok Choy, garlic, towel gourd, etc. When we taste the vegetables planted by our parents and offer praises that the vegetables are delicious and organic, they are really delighted. Zhu Yanqun's mother has put it that planting vegetables resembles planting flowers, in that both serve as ornamental plants; planting vegetables is, however, better, in that vegetables are of great value as food. Such labor as planting vegetables is really good, and deserves to live long.

## 共同语言

酒逢知己千杯少,话不投机半句多。可见,共同语言对于人际关系的相处,是何等重要。子女和父母亲的关系是亲属关系,当然也是人际关系,所以,共同语言同样是不可或缺的。"文革"期间,因政治观点、思想倾向不一,夫妻离异、兄弟反目、父子不睦的时有所闻。现在我们提倡和而不同,允许有不同政见,但思想接近一点,共同语言多一点的人在一起,总是容易相处一点,相处起来总会舒服一点。子女和父母因为各为独立的个体,所以有所不同是正常的,也是必然的。因为都是人,又同种同语,又受家庭影响,所以共同点也不乏。求同存异是上策,平时多说共同语言是相处之艺术,也是孝顺的一种表现。

反对放鞭炮,是我们和朱艳群父母的共同语言,每当春节,耳闻窗外此起彼伏的鞭炮噪音,我们就在一起说放鞭炮的三大坏处:一为污染环境,二为事故隐患,三为浪费钱财。我们说,不放鞭炮当然谈不上有多少好,但可以避免上述的几点不好,所以希望政府禁止。

不信教,也是我们和朱艳群父母的共同语言,我们也屡说不厌。我们说,信基督教是一种信仰,信伊斯兰教是一种信仰,信佛教是一种信仰。不信教,也是一种信仰,而且更是真正属于自己的信仰。世界上现有的各式各样的教,都是我们的古人创造的,并不是哪一个今人发明的。对于教,有人信,有人半信半疑,有人一概不信。信者是人云亦云,半信者是无力判断,不信者才是有自己主见的,货真价实的有信仰者。

子女和父母在一起说说共同语言,是一种比天伦之乐更乐的乐,更高级的乐,也是填平代沟的有效方式。自然,孝,也在其中了。

# A Common Language

When you chat over wine with a friend who knows you well, a thousand toasts are far too few; when you chat with a person with whom you have no common interests, you don't bother to utter half a sentence. Obviously, a common language is of vital importance to maintaining interpersonal relationship. Child-parent relationship is a kind of kinship, and of course interpersonal. So, a common language is indispensible as well. During "the Cultural Revolution", it's not uncommon to hear about cases that couples divorce, brothers break up and father and son are at odds as a result of disagreements on political views and ideological tendencies. Now we advocate harmony but not sameness and allow for different political views. However, it's surely much easier and more comfortable for people of more common interests to get along. Since children and parents are independent individuals, it's normal and unavoidable for differences to occur. However, being human beings, and of the same kinship and language, children and parents also have some in common. Thus seeking common ground while reserving differences is the best policy. Using the common language more often is the art of getting along, and the embodiment of filial piety.

Objecting to setting off firecrackers is the common language between Zhu Yanqun's parents and us. When it's Spring Festival, hearing the noise of firecrackers outdoors one after another, we will always have a discussion on the three major shortcomings of firecrackers: First, it pollutes the environment, second, it poses potential accident threats, and third, it wastes money. We think, to stop setting off firecrackers can't be counted as something good, but it can avoid the above-mentioned shortcomings, so we hope the government can ban that.

Not having religious beliefs is the common language and also a frequently talked-about topic among us. In our opinion, believing in Islam is a belief, believing in Buddhism is a belief, too. Not being religious is also a belief. And it's more of a belief that truly belongs to oneself. The currently existing religions worldwide were all created by our ancestors rather than the contemporaries. Of religions, some are full believers, some half believers and others atheists. Believers echo the views of others, half believers are incapable of making judgments, and only atheists are inner-directed, real believers.

Children and parents getting together and sharing a common language is more pleasant and advanced than family happiness. It's also an effective way to bridge the generation gap. And filial piety is surely embodied in it.

# 让父母作点主

古今中外，人总是喜欢作主的。老百姓要当家作主，就闹民主；统治者要独裁——一人作主，就搞专制。

为什么要作主？因为作主的背后有利益。人民要当家作主，是想保护自身的利益不受侵犯，独裁者要替民作主，是想剥夺人民的利益为己有。阶级斗争人民胜利了，就建立民主国家；独裁者胜利了，就建立专制国家。

在千千万万个家庭里，常常是子女未成年的时候，父母是一家之主，大事小事由父母作主。子女成年以后，尤其是结婚以后，父母就作不了子女的主了，只能"自扫门前雪"。待到父母年事已高，住到子女那里去，则"主权"归子女，只有建议权、"拍手权"，没有决策权了。

未成年的子女在家里没有作主权，应该没什么不舒服，因为他们从未有过这种权，以及这种权带来的好处，如同无官无权的人退休以后没有失落感，退休叫做享受。只有专制社会的官退了以后才难过，随着权力的失去，势也没了，利也没了，甚至旁人的尊重也没了。

人老了，住到子女那里去，虽有血缘相连，亲情可依，可少了当家作主，未免滋味不佳。朱艳群深明老人心，体贴入微，想方设法满足父母在家里有所作主的心理需求。

我们家有个习惯,每隔一年半载,要将家里的家具摆设换换位,如背对窗的沙发改成面对窗,靠东边墙的餐桌放到靠西边墙,楼上的窗帘和楼下的窗帘对换。凡此种种什么时候变、改、换,我们全让朱艳群的父母作主。在我们家,日常生活中让老人作主的事,突出的还有买什么样的菜。明天家里吃什么菜,隔夜朱艳群总会让母亲写在纸上。只要"菜单"上的市场里有,必定在第二天的餐桌上。

　　邓小平曾对英国人说,中国人民解放军在香港驻军,是主权的象征,不容商量。朱艳群让年老的父母在家里作主家具的摆设、吃菜的品种之类,大概也有某种象征的意义吧。

# Leaving Decisions to Parents

At all times, be it at home or abroad, people always like to make decisions. When ordinary people want to be masters of the country and make decisions, they will press for democracy; when the governor wants to dictate— to make decisions all by himself, he will implement autocracy.

Why to make decisions? There are interests behind. Ordinary people want to make decisions so they can protect their own interests from violation. And the dictator wants to make decisions for people so he can expropriate people's interests. When people win in the class struggle, a democratic country will be established; when the dictator wins, an autocratic country will get founded.

In most families, before children enter adulthood, parents are always the masters, making both big and small decisions. After children grow into adulthood, especially after they get married, parents can no longer make decisions for their children. Rather, they "sweep the snow in front of their door" and make decisions for themselves only. But when parents get old and move to their children's home, the "decision-making right" shifts to the children. Parents then have rights to suggest and "applaud", but no right to decide.

Children before adulthood are supposed to be comfortable with having no right to decide in the families, in that they have no prior experiences of enjoying this right and the benefits that ensue. It's just like retirees who, with no official titles and power, don't have a feeling of loss. For them, retirement equals enjoyment. Only officials from an autocratic society have a hard time after retirement. With the loss of power, gone are their influence, interests and even others' respect.

When the elderly move to live with their children, although they are from the same kinship and have family bond in between, the old are likely to feel uncomfortable with not being masters of the family. Zhu Yanqun knows clearly what the elderly think and is extremely considerate to them, doing everything possible to meet her parents' psychological demands of making some decisions in the family.

It's a routine in our family that every one year or so, we will change positions of the furniture at home, such as repositioning the sofa with its back to the window to face the window, placing the dining table against the west wall which is originally against the east wall, and swapping the upstairs and downstairs curtains. We leave all such decisions to Zhu Yanqun's parents as when to change, place and swap interior furniture and decorations. Another typical type of decisions that we leave to parents are about dishes to buy. Zhu Yanqun always lets her mother put down on the paper names of the dishes to eat the next day. So long as what's on the "menu" can be found in the market, it will surely appear on the table the next day.

Deng Xiaoping used to tell the British that it's a symbol of sovereignty for People's Liberation Army to station troops in Hong Kong and it allows no bargaining. That Zhu Yanqun leaves decisions about layout of furniture and varieties of dishes to the elderly parents could be of symbolic significance too.

# 母亲的远亲

媒体报道，90后女局长王茜被免职，其父王达武受党内警告处分，被免去湖南省发改委重大项目办公室主任职务。

90后的王茜被免职，不是因为她当局长后犯了什么大错，而是因为她压根儿没有当局长的资格，她的官位是通过非正常途径获取的。其父王达武受处分、被免职，不是受女儿株连，而是他"运作"女儿当官。

读了这条新闻，感觉不错，感觉自己没有生活在太不好的时代和太不好的国家。不是吗？在这个世界上，还有那么一些国家，父亲的职务是可以由子女顶替的，哪怕这个父亲是一国之首，肩负领导全国人民的重任。在这样的国度里，利用权力让90后的子女当一个什么局长，根本不会有问题，要是谁反对，这个反对者不被抓起来才怪呢！所以，活在今天的中国，还是庆幸的。

一个省的发改委重大项目办公室主任，是一个小得不能再小的"七品芝麻官"，不过他当得一定很舒服，于是己所欲施于女，设法让女儿也来当个官，然后以官取利。王达武爱女之心无可非议，可他犯了一个低级错误，他把那官位当成自家的私产了，随意可以给女儿。对王达武，我有个建议，建议他辞官下海创办民营企业，到时他赚了钱，可以给女儿，或者安排女儿到公司来当个总经理。这样既给了女儿利，又没人说闲话。

还是朱艳群聪明,自办企业自作主,不仅让老母当"文秘",还听母亲的话,把母亲的几个远亲招到公司来上班。这几个远亲,有的是朱艳群的表妹,有的是朱艳群的表外甥女,如果按照公司的招工条件,她们是进不来的,可朱艳群以为,自己创办企业,不全为了赚取利润,还有孝敬父母的成分在,所以母亲前来"开后门",要她照顾远亲的时候,她二话没说照办了。

# Mum's Distant Relatives

It's reported that Wang Qian, the "post-90s" female director, has been deposed and Wang Dawu, her father, has been given the inner-party disciplinary warning and removed from his post of Director of Hunan Province Development and Reform Commission Major Projects Office.

The "post-90s" Wang Qian is deposed not because she has made any blunder, but because she is completely not qualified for the post. Her official position was secured by irregular means. And her father was given disciplinary punishment and deposed not because he was implicated by his daughter but because he had "manipulated power" to put his daughter to the official position.

Reading the news, I feel good. We are not living in too bad times and in too bad countries, aren't we? In the world, there are still a number of countries where father's post can be replaced by his children, even if the father is the head of the country, playing a prominent role in the leadership of the whole nation. In such countries, there is no problem at all for a father to wield power and put his "post-90s" child to a director's position. I'll be much mistaken if any opponent of this doesn't get arrested. Thus, I feel very lucky living in today's China.

A director of provincial Development and Reform Commission Major Projects Office is the lowest by rank. Anyway, he must have been very comfortable with being that. So he puts what he himself wants on his daughter, managing to make his daughter an official so that his daughter can make profits. Wang Dawu's love for his daughter is not to blame, but he has committed a low-level error, regarding his position as private properties, which he can give away to his daughter at will. To Wang Dawu, I would suggest he should resign the official post and establish his own business. When he makes money, he can either give it to his daughter or arrange for his daughter to be General Manager of the company. This will not only benefit his daughter but stop others' gossip.

Zhu Yanqun is obviously more intelligent. She has founded her own company and made all decisions independently. She appointed her mom as "secretary", and followed her advice, recruiting some distant relatives of her mother as staff of her company. Of these distant relatives, some are Zhu Yanqun's cousins, some are daughters of her cousins'. Given the company's recruitment conditions, they will be denied admission. But in Zhu Yanqun's opinion, she has opened business not only to make profits, but also to honor her parents. So when her mother came to "open the back door", asking her to recruit these relatives, she always said nothing and did it.

# 不一样的饼

中国的月亮和外国的月亮没区别，一样地圆，一样地大。

中国的饼和西方国家的饼不一样，中国的饼饼里有馅，西方国家的饼饼面有料。中国的"里"，反映了中国人的含蓄；西方国家的"外"，反映了西方人的直白。

中国南方的饼和中国北方的饼也有差异，南方的饼甜的多，北方的饼咸的多。吃甜的南方人性温和，吃咸的北方人性刚烈。据食物专家说，吃甜，利于心情舒畅。南方人的饼也小有差别，有的放葱，有的不放。不同的人吃不同的饼，从一个侧面体现人与人是不同的。

我们家对饼的喜好分成了三派，朱艳群喜吃加葱的饼，女儿无所谓加葱不加葱，我和朱艳群母亲不吃加葱的饼。众口难调，怎么处理呢？只要母亲不在，朱艳群一律在饼里加葱，说是这样香，口感好，还利于健康，理由一大堆，全然不顾我的反对，反正女儿是中间派。但只要她母亲参与吃饼，那饼里必定无葱。由此可见，朱艳群唯母为重，重过自己。

# Cakes of Difference

There is no difference between the Chinese moon and the foreign moon. They are of the same shape and size.

There is difference between Chinese cakes and western cakes. Chinese cakes have stuffing inside the cake, while western cakes have topping outside on the crust. The Chinese "inside" has reflected the Chinese implicitness, while the western "outside" has reflected the western straightforwardness.

Even in China, there is difference between cakes in the south and cakes in the north. Cakes in the south are mostly sweet-flavored, and cakes in the north are mostly salty. The southerners eat more sweet foods and tend to have gentle temperament, while the northerners who love salty foods have strong temperament. Eating desserts, as is claimed by food experts, helps maintain the ease of mind. And there is also minor difference among cakes in the south, some with spring onion and some without. Different people like different cakes, which partly shows that people differ from one to another.

In my family, people's preferences fall into three categories. Zhu Yanqun likes cakes with spring onion, my daughter doesn't care, and Zhu Yanqun's mother and I don't eat cakes with spring onion. It's really hard to cater to all tastes. How to cope with that? So long as her mother is not present, Zhu

Yanqun always puts spring onion in the cakes, saying that it's savory and tasty and is good for health. She will present a list of reasons, completely ignoring my objection. Anyway, my daughter is the centrist. However, as long as her mother joins us to eat cakes, there is definitely no spring onion inside. This surely shows that Zhu Yanqun places her mother's demands above her own.

# 甜食的功能

小时候玩蟋蟀,让蟋蟀吃辣椒,以使它性凶猛,牙坚硬,斗败对手。

喜欢吃辣的湖南人和四川人性格多刚烈,连女性也不例外,湘妹子、川妹子,都有辣的味道。喜欢吃甜食的江南人则性温婉,尤其是女人,不会发飙,只会撒娇。可见,食物跟性格有关,不同的食物造就不同的性格。至于哪种性格优,哪种性格劣,则很难区分,似乎也不必区分。好像战争年代,更需要刚烈性格的人,所以湖南四川出了不少将领。和平年代还是温婉一些好吧,利于谈判,利于和谐,所以江浙一带经济发展较快,社会相对稳定。

甜食另有一大好处,就是食之利于心情开朗。据说,平时喜食甜品的人,很少患忧郁症。朱艳群的母亲是个弱女子,又多读了一点文学书,所以常会多愁善感,每遇烦心事,就生出些许忧郁来。针对这一情况,朱艳群一方面多说让母亲开心的话,多做让母亲开心的事,尽量减少母亲愁和忧郁的来源。另一方面,常弄些甜食给母亲吃,如巧克力、如水蜜桃、如小笼包、如甜粥、如带甜的年糕,等等。

朱艳群的母亲深有体会地说:"年轻时,甜食吃得少,悲观情绪多,如今多吃了甜食,好像乐观起来了。"

# The Functions of Desserts

In the childhood game of cricket fighting, we always fed crickets with chili to make them more ferocious and hard-toothed, so they can defeat the rivals.

Chili-lovers like people born or native in Hunan and Sichuan mostly have staunch characters. Females are no exception. "Hunan sisters" and "Sichuan sisters" are all spicy girls. Dessert-lovers like people born or native in regions south of the Yangtze River have more gentle temperament. Women in particular won't fly into a rage but react in a mild and gentle way. Obviously, food has something to do with temperaments; different foods make different temperaments. As for which temperament is superior to another, it's really hard and unnecessary to distinguish. For instance, in the war years which call for people of strong temperament, Hunan and Sichuan have brought up many generals. However, in the years of peace, acting in a mild and gentle way contributes to negotiation and harmony, so in regions of Zhejiang Province and Jiangsu Province, economy is developed more rapidly and the society is more stable.

Another benefit of eating desserts is that it helps maintain optimistic mood. It's said that dessert-lovers rarely suffer from depression. Zhu Yanqun's mother is a typically feminine lady and loves reading literature, so she often appears to be sentimental. Every time she encounters bothering things, she gets caught up in sentiment. Considering this, on the one hand, Zhu Yanqun speaks words and does things that delight her mother, to minimize the generation of her mother's worries and sentiment; on the other hand, she often prepares some desserts for her mother, such as chocolates, peaches, small steamed buns with stuffing, sweet congee, glutinous rice cake with sweet dipping, and so on.

Zhu Yanqun's mother has had much feeling about that and said, "In my youth, I ate few desserts and had much pessimistic emotion. Now that I eat more desserts, I've become more optimistic."

# 取名

每个人都有自己的名字,可名字多有别人给取,少有自己给自己取名的。

因为名字不是自己所取,所以名字的含义代表不了自己的理念,可以此能知晓取名者的价值观、品味和追求。女儿高韵洌的名字是我取的。韵其外,洌其内,外柔内刚。有漂亮的外貌,又有理念、思想、个性。如今的女儿果其然,她也喜欢这个名字。我有个50后的好朋友,他给儿子取名驾风,意即不随波逐流,不跟风,不盲目跟着领头羊走,而要有主见,不跟风而驾风。

孔子说,孝敬父母,初等的是赡养其身,中等的是不使其忧,高等的是尊重其人格,愉悦其心。朱艳群深明此理,总会想出些让父母开心,让父母觉得自己有价值的事来。让年老的母亲给外孙女取未来子女的名字,就是朱艳群的一招。朱艳群说,让母亲取名,一方面是发挥母亲文字功底好的特长;另一方面是以此体现对母亲的尊重,让母亲活得更有尊严。

朱艳群的母亲果然乐意接受给"第四代"取名的使命,她半个月来日思夜想,终于取出了让家人人人满意的名字——如生男,取名"境远";如生女,取名"境遥"。朱艳群说:"境远、境遥好,意即好家境长远。"女儿说:"这个名字意境悠远,有想头,比较从容,也好听。"我说:"这个名字,既朴素,又优雅;既通俗,又深刻。"

听了我们的赞美,老人笑得比吃了糖还甜。

# Giving Names

Everybody has his or her own name. But mostly, the name is given by others rather than by himself or herself.

Now that names are not given by the name-owners themselves, the implication of the names can't reflect their own ideas. However, the values, tastes and goals of the name-givers can be reflected. My daughter's name "Gao Yunlie" is given by me. Literally, it means "charm outward, cool inward". It actually implies the girl is supposed to have both good looks and ideals, independent thinking and individualities. Now my daughter has lived up to the name, and she loves the name, too. A good friend of mine, who was born in 1950s, has named his son "Jia Feng", which means not drifting with the current, not following the wind and not going after the bellwether blindly, but having independent thinking, namely, riding the wind.

As Confucius has put it, to show filial piety to parents, the low-level requirement is to support parents, the more advanced is not to make parents worried, and the high-level requirement is to respect parents' personalities and delight them spiritually. Zhu Yanqun is well aware of it and often comes up with things for parents to do, which make them feel pleased and valued. To let her elderly mother find names for the granddaughter's future children is one of Zhu Yanqun's good ideas. Zhu Yanqun has explained, on the one hand, it can give full play to her mother's strengths in writing, and on the other hand, it can make her mother live with more respect and dignity.

As expected, Zhu Yanqun's mother accepted the mission with pleasure. She spent half a month racking her brain and finally came up with the names satisfying everybody in the family— "Jing Yuan" for a boy and "Jing Yao" for a girl. Zhu Yanqun said, "Both have good implications, meaning good family situations for ever." My daughter said, "The names have nice artistic conception, are thought-provoking and sounds pleasing to ears." I said, "The names are both simple and elegant; both popular and profound."

Hearing our compliments, the elderly lady smiled a most sweet smile.

# 替母购书

投其所好是中性词,看用在什么地方,用好了是褒义词,用错地方则是贬义词。投领导所好是拍马屁,通常是不好的。投人民所好是为人民服务,应当提倡。

朱艳群的母亲喜欢看书,朱艳群便常常替母亲购书,可谓投其所好。这样的投其所好好不好,不言自明。

朱艳群替母亲购的书,都会写上"女儿赠阅"四个字。一个节假日,闲来无事,我在岳母的书房里清点"女儿赠阅",一数,超过了一百本。这里不妨列出部分书目,看看朱艳群在选书问题上是如何投母所好的。刘再复与林岗合著的《传统与中国人》、刘再复的《人性诸相》。钱理群的《活着的意义》。易中天的《中国的男人和女人》、《品三国》、《品人录》、《我山之石》、《书生傻气》、《公民心事》。章诒和的《往事并不如烟》、《杨氏女》、《刘氏女》。罗银胜的《顾准再思录》、《顾准评传》。王文元的《人类的自我毁灭》。黎鸣的《老不死的传统》。贺雄飞的《信仰与危机》。渡边淳一的《失乐园》、《复乐园》。《在北大听讲座》整整21册。

# Buying Books for Mum

"Catering to others' preferences" is neutral and hinges on contexts. In some cases, it's positive, while in other cases, it's negative. Catering to the officials' preferences is bootlicking and therefore discouraged, while catering to the public preferences is serving the public and deserves to be encouraged.

Zhu Yanqun's mother likes reading, so Yanqun often buys books for her, which can be described as catering to her mother's preference for books. Whether this kind of catering is good or not is really self-evident.

On the books she bought for her mother, Zhu Yanqun always writes down the characters of "Sent by daughter, for reading". The other day in holidays when I was not engaged in anything, in my mother-in-law's study I had counted the number of books Yanqun bought for her and found the total number has exceeded one hundred. Here I might as well make an incomplete list of book titles, and find out how Zhu Yanqun has catered to her mother's preferences in book selection. *Tradition and the Chinese*, co-authored by Liu Zaifu and Lin Gang, and *Aspects of Human Nature* by Liu Zaifu. *Reasons of Being* authored by Qian Liqun. *Men and Women in China*, *Savoring the Three Kingdoms*, *Savoring Human Nature*, *Stones from My Mountain*, *Bookish Scholars* and *What's in Citizens' Mind* by Yi Zhongtian. *The Past*

*Is Not Gone Like Smoke*, *Lady of the Yang Family* and *Lady of the Liu Family* by Zhang Yihe. *Thinking of Gu Zhun*, and *Biography of Gu zhun* by Luo Yinsheng. *Self-destruction of Human Beings* by Wang Wenyuan. *The Tradition of Being Old But Lively* by Li Ming. *Trust and Crisis* by He Xiongfei. *Paradise Lost* and *Paradise Regained* by Junichi Watanabe. And the 21 volume *Going to Lectures in Peking University*.

# 松散的大家庭

大有大的好处,小有小的好处。同样,大也有大的坏处,小也有小的坏处。

家庭的大小之好坏亦如是。小家庭,可以自由自在,清清静静,这是小家庭的好处。大家庭,可以热热闹闹,其乐融融,这是大家庭的好处。

人是群体动物,所以要大家庭;人要追求个性,所以要小家庭。

我们夫妇、一个女儿加上朱艳群的父母,五口之家,比之小家庭大了一点,比之过去那种四世同堂,小了一点。朱艳群的父母有四个子女,老人平时和我们一起生活。在老人的感觉里,只要不是和所有的子女在一起,总是小家一个,但在当今社会,要组建四世同堂的大家庭不切实际。

为了解决香港、澳门归国问题,邓小平发明了一国两制。为了兼顾家庭小有小的好处,大有大的好处,朱艳群发明了平时小家庭、节假日大家庭,或曰松散的大家庭。就是让她父母平时和我们一起过小家庭生活,到了周末或节日,则常常组织家庭大聚会,把哥哥姐姐及家人请来,和老人一起过四世同堂的大家庭生活。

松散的大家庭,有分又有合,舍去了大和小的弊病,获取了大和小的好处。一国两制是因国制宜,实事求是。平时小家庭、周末大家庭——松散的大家庭,是因家制宜,实事求是。这样的模式,既遂了老人的心,又合了子女的愿,两全其美。愚以为,大可推广之。

# A Big Loosely-structured Family

Being big can be both good and bad. So is being small. This rule also applies to the size of families. Small families always bring more freedom and tranquility. It's the good side of small families. However, big families can ensure more liveliness and enjoyment, which is the good side of big families.

Humans are social animals living in groups, so we need big families; humans also pursue individuality, so we need small families as well.

We couple, our daughter and Zhu Yanqun's parents make up the five-member family. It's bigger than small families, and smaller than those traditional families consisting of four generations. Zhu's parents have four children, but the parents usually live with us. In their eyes, so long as they don't live with all the children, it is no more than a small family. But in today's society, it's really impractical to form a big four-generation family.

In order to solve the return problems of Hong Kong and Macau, Deng Xiaoping has devised the "One Country, Two Systems" policy. And to balance the advantages and disadvantages of big and small families, Zhu has established the practice of "small families on weekdays, big families on weekends and holidays", or the so-called "loose, big family". Namely, her parents usually live a small-family life with us, but on weekends or holidays, we always invite brothers, sisters and other relatives to come over and live the four-generation family life together with our parents.

There is separation and union in big loosely-structured families, which avoids the disadvantages of being big and being small, and keeps the advantages of both. The "One Country, Two Systems" policy is practical and realistic, adapting to the country's conditions. Similarly, the "small families on weekdays, big families on weekends" mode adapts to the family's conditions, being practical and realistic. It caters to both the elderly parents and young children, so, in my humble opinion, it deserves being popularized.

# 照相

物理学有个原理,任何东西通过一个管道,它一定会或多或少损失一点。有个笑话,说是城西杀了一只鸡,传话传到城东,成了杀了一个娘。

照相,虽有"两我"之说,但毕竟"过了一道",与真实的自己总有那么一些区别,故有上照不上照之说。尤其那个写真,大有写假的味道,与原先的样子相去甚远。说白了,"过了一道"就是打折,原先美的,变得不那么美了,原先丑的,变得不那么丑了,因为美和丑均打了折。可见,美人写真是吃亏的,丑人写真是占便宜的。

根据照相就是打折的原理,老人照相也是划算的,经过一番修饰,取一个好的角度,面带微笑,相片上的老人可以显得比实际年龄小一点。朱艳群不知是缘于此,还是别的什么原因,很是喜欢给母亲照相,除了带母亲去照相馆拍照,还陪母亲去风景区拍照,有时在家里,又用手机随意替母亲拍几张。

朱艳群给母亲照相,还会让母亲不断地换衣服,好似让她当时装模特,以此增添拍摄过程的快乐和成照后的效果。所以,无论是拍照的时候,还是过后看到照片,朱艳群的母亲总是一脸灿烂,如此地开心,唯有精神上的满足方能获取。

人是需要信心的,少年时需要学习能力的信心,中青年时需要社交能力和工作能力的信心,人老了以后,则需要对自身生命力的信心。老人拍一点好的照片,看看照片上的自己神清气爽,精神饱满,是可以增强对生命力的信心的。朱艳群让母亲多多照相,孝心使然也。

# Photo-taking

It's a principle in physics that once anything gets through a channel, it will surely suffer loss more or less. As a joke has it, a cock gets killed in the west of the city, but when the message gets spread to the east, it becomes "a mother gets killed".

Although photo-taking is always associated with "dual I", however, after all, the person has been "photographed", so there is surely some difference between the photographed self and the true self. That's why there is a saying of "being photogenic or not". Especially the "writing true" (portrait photograph) is usually far different from the original image, so it can simply be called "writing false". To put it plainly, "being photographed" equals discounting. Namely, what's originally beautiful gets not so beautiful and what's originally ugly gets not so ugly, because beauty and ugliness both get discounted. As is seen, the beautiful are put at a disadvantage when photographed, while the ugly are made advantageous when photographed.

According to the principle of "photographing is discounting", it's a good deal for the elderly to be photographed. Dressed up, from a favorable perspective, and with a smile, the elderly seem much younger in photographs than in real life. Maybe for this or another reason, Zhu Yanqun likes taking photos for her mother. She takes her to the photo studio, and also to the scenic spots for photos. Sometimes, she also casually takes photos for her mother at home with her cell phone.

When Zhu Yanqun takes photos for her mother, she will suggest her put on different clothes, as if she were made a fashion model, in order to enhance the pleasure of photographing and the effects of imaging. As a result, whether when she is being photographed or when afterwards she sees the photos, Zhu Yanqun's mother is always beaming. Such happiness can only be secured with spiritual satisfaction.

All humans need confidence. Teenagers need confidence in the learning abilities, the young and the mid-aged need confidence in the social skills and working capabilities, and the elderly need confidence in their own vitality. When the elderly see themselves refreshed and energetic in photos, it helps enhance their confidence in vitality. Zhu Yanqun's attempts to take photos for her mother as much as possible are indeed triggered by nothing but her filial piety.

**图书在版编目（CIP）数据**

精养父母实验报告：汉英对照 / 高鸣著；张宏，姜琪瑶译．—上海：文汇出版社，2013.2
ISBN 978-7-5496-0833-1

Ⅰ．①精… Ⅱ．①高… ②张… ③姜… Ⅲ．①故事－作品集－中国－当代－汉、英 Ⅳ．①I247.8

中国版本图书馆CIP数据核字（2013）第024292号

# 精养父母实验报告

著作权人 / 高　鸣
责任编辑 / 吴　斐
装帧设计 / 周　丹

出版发行 / 文匯出版社
　　　　　上海市威海路755号
　　　　　（邮政编码200041）
印刷装订 / 苏州华美教育印刷有限公司
版　　次 / 2013年2月第1版
印　　次 / 2013年2月第1次印刷
开　　本 / 787×1092　1/16
字　　数 / 160千
印　　张 / 12
印　　数 / 1—10000

ISBN 978-7-5496-0833-1
定　　价 / 40.00元